REBECKA LASSEN

Socially Accepted Intuition

Lina,

I'm so glad we sat next to each other during class! Excited for your book — no matter when it comes out!

Editor: Kathleen Tracy

Book Design Cover: Pradeep Premalal

Author's Photo: Michael Hamerlind Photography

First edition

ISBN: 978-0-578-21938-7

This book was professionally typeset on Reedsy.
Find out more at reedsy.com

To Laurie Baughn.
Someone I will never have the privilege to meet
but will forever be grateful for her divine intervening.
Thank you for bringing me Ingrid.

Contents

Acknowledgement

If it wasn't for Ingrid Koller this book would not exist. First and foremost I thank her endless wisdom and encouragement. She was able to help me through the many emotional breakdowns while writing this book. Thank you, Ingrid.

Second, I thank my family. My logical, analytical, skeptical husband has endured a lot. Even though he didn't necessarily believe in what I was doing, he believed in me. Thank you. And thank you to my kids. Someone asked my daughter if mommy plays ponies with her. She said, "Not much; she's always reading." Thank you for at least calling me out for something good and not just drinking wine. I'm so excited to play ponies more! And yes, Legos too, Victor.

Thank you to my siblings and parents. Thank you for allowing me to publish part of our family's history. It's not all glorious, but who cares? It's who we are, and we are fucking awesome!

Thank you to my editor Kathleen Tracy. Thank you for allowing me to keep my voice, but still make me sound like I actually know what I'm doing. Thank you!

Thank you to my launch team, Jody Haseleu, Ashley Arneson, Kayla Erickson, Jennifer Rechtfertig, Amanda Meidinger, Brittany Miskowiec, Rachel Schaub, Trinity Potts, Serina Nelson, and Heidi Carter. You all believed in me and my message enough to take some of your invaluable time to share it. For the bottom of my heart, thank you all.

A special thank you to Rachel Schaub. I can't even guess how many times you read sections of my book before they were even close to being ready. Your constant encouragement—but mostly humorous gif and meme messages—got me through this process. Thank you!

To everyone that read my book before and gave me feedback and allowed me to tell part of their story—Jane and Tim Paskvan, Trisha Alber, Sam Fenton, Zack Anderson—thank you all. Thank you everyone for being part of this with me.

Author's Note

Socially Accepted Intuition has many stories written based on my memory, along with the recollections of a few others I consulted along the way. Memory is malleable; everyone is susceptible to false recalls, remembering events differently from the exact way they actually happened.

It's why I highly recommend you check out Malcolm Gladwell's *Revisionist History* podcast. Every episode re-examines something from the past—an event, a person, an idea, even a song—and asks whether we got it right the first time. Specifically, he had featured memory in a two-part series, *A Polite Word for Liar* and *Free Brian Williams*. He uses a story about a world-class harmonica player raiding a Nazi safe house and the 2015 controversy over Brian Williams' claim of being shot at in a helicopter in Iraq to help us understand how memory functions.

Gladwell does an excellent job of explaining that all humans have shitty memories. He explains it more gracefully than that, but that's the gist of it. You should listen. Just do it after you read my book. Or just make sure you come back. I'd hate that you spent your money on my book just for a podcast recommendation.

Intuition: The ability to understand something immediately, without the need for conscious reasoning. A thing that one knows or considers likely from instinctive feeling rather than conscious reasoning.

The Universe: All of space and time and their contents, including planets, stars, galaxies, and all other forms of matter and energy; an infinite wisdom, a higher power, a something bigger than human.

1

Introduction

I'm from North Dakota. With this statement alone you're probably making a few assumptions about me. Some would be correct. I do enjoy being outdoors unless there's a sub-zero wind chill. Screw that shit. I like gardening, despite my inability to actually grow anything. I also hate deer enough to want to hunt them down on a yearly basis. This hatred stems from them eating my garden. I mean, venison is good too, but the motivation is mostly hatred.

Some of your assumptions would be wrong. I am not a Republican. I guess I don't consider myself a Democrat either. I'm one of those people who take an online survey the day before voting that matches me to candidates based on my political stances. A quick Google search of each matched candidate to make sure they haven't ax-murdered anyone and I'm good. Sure, these surveys don't cover the local candidates, but let's be honest; how often do judges really have a huge political battle?

Early on I knew I wasn't *really* a North Dakotan. Being a *Nodak* just never felt right to me. I wasn't able to articulate what the off feeling was until one morning in the summer of 2017. I woke up at 3:00 a.m. and had an overwhelming urge to start writing a book. That urge would not go away, so as much as I love to sleep, I knew I had to get up and write.

I had no idea what I was doing. I took English-12 in high school instead of Honors English because I was lazy and didn't care to write that much. I had a tiny vocabulary. I overused commas—and still do—and skipped words entirely. My dear friend, Ingrid, (who most likely took Honors English) reviewed my work each week and sent me corrections. As I continued to write, some amazing things happened. Eventually the red, squiggly lines in my word document became fewer and fewer. Thesaurus.com became my best friend. And the best part was, for your sake and mine, I figured out what this book is about—intuition. I want to help you understand more about intuition and learn how to access this superpower.

I've always had intuition but didn't understand it. There was always a little voice or that feeling that warned me, even directed me, but I couldn't follow it. How would I explain to my friends I didn't want to drive out to the lake because of a horrible feeling I had? There was nothing logical I could say to them about this sudden, tremendous fear I felt.

How could I tell anyone that I refused to go back to that one house because of a strange encounter I had. I told my mom about it, and she calmly explained how annoying that ghost was since it would follow my mom around and mess with things. Great. Not only would people think I'm crazy but that my mom is batshit crazy too.

I had to squash those feelings and encounters deep down inside so people wouldn't see I was different. In small-town North Dakota different is bad. Different gets you tossed out of your tribe and left to fend for yourself. Normal people can form a pack together and survive.

I wanted people to accept me. I wanted to be normal, so I tried to be that "normal" person. I wanted to fit in with society's rules just enough so I could become something. I had this idea that if I wanted to be a person who listened to my intuition, I had to embrace a hippy, crunchy lifestyle that I absolutely didn't want. I must confess there was a brief time when that hippy '70s style came back in my tween years. I got myself a cool, inflatable chair covered in yellow, pink, and soft-blue daisy flowers. I wore big bell-bottom jeans with iron-on patches of daisies and peace signs. Thank goodness that phase passed for me because it wasn't really me. Since then there has been no tie-dyed apparel in my wardrobe. I want world peace but don't care to throw the universal peace sign around. Patchouli incense is not my thing either. Ick. My mother wore a leather fringe jacket in her senior picture—also not my thing.

I'm not saying those things are bad. If tie-dyed T-shirts and incense are your thing, cool. Awesome. Totally rad, man. I'm just saying they aren't for me. For the rest of us, I'm telling you, there is an in-between. It's not just black or white. I think that's why I never fit in. Only later in my thirties did I find out there is a balanced, beautiful world in-between crunchy and socially accepted. The secret of finding this world is our intuition. We don't need all the fringe and frills we have too-long associated with being intuitive.

It took me a long time to find this balanced world. Growing up I tried hard to be accepted by family and friends. Acceptance is literally all I wanted. It's what any kid wants. It's safe to be accepted. In fact it's a biological instinct humans developed for survival. If your tribe didn't like you, they kicked you out of the cave then you would get eaten by a saber-toothed tiger. I didn't want to be eaten by a saber-toothed tiger. After every weird, awkward thing I said or did, I waited for the small-town tribe to grab their clubs and chase me out. I'd be a delicious snack for the saber-toothed tiger.

Luckily after a few life changes, something took hold of me when I was seventeen. Without realizing it I signed the dotted line for what would be a free trip to Iraq to fight a war, followed by a fourteen-year career in the Army National Guard. Then without my full awareness, I got thrown into a holistic living world. In a matter of a few short years, I've come to a deep understanding of how my intuition, the Universe, and myself work together for a bigger purpose.

Once I combined my desire to be accepted and successful with my logical, military mindset, I learned how to approach my intuitive side with a skeptical but open mindset. I now understand and see the widespread epidemic of mistreated intuition. It's very distressing to witness people shut down that inner voice when that is exactly the answer they are looking for. Intuition is a key element for our success and psychological well-being.

I've come to understand is that we need to access our intuition now more than ever. We are forced to interpret misleading headlines and are continually fed information from social media sources that are just flat out false.

Don't believe everything you read on the internet. — *Abe Lincoln.*

We need to turn to our inner truth to understand the real truth of our world.

I think it's important to understand I'm not asking anyone to change any beliefs or religion. No need to go vegan. Don't buy up all the iron-on patches at Claire's, either—unless that's your thing. (I'm told that's a thing again.) You do you. Everyone has this superpower, waiting to be harnessed—intuition. I just want to take away the bullshit from some common aspects of intuition and give you some basic tools to access it.

Socially Accepted Intuition is a fun, humorous take on our desires to become socially accepted but also be true to ourselves. This story is about overcoming what we think we should be and learning to trust the path that will lead us to where our purpose really is. Give yourself the green light to accept intuitive thoughts that may not seem to make sense. Learn how using your intuition can bring you to a place of acceptance. There are only two things you need to tap into your intuition: keep reading and learn to trust yourself.

2

The Forty Is Stupid

I grew up on our family farm just outside of Dickey, North Dakota, population forty-one. A big bag of Totino's has more pizza rolls than Dickey has people. I'm the youngest of four. Many of the assumptions about being the baby of the family are true about me, so feel free to assume away. My parents divorced when I was five, and my earliest childhood memory is our mom telling us the news as she sat in her '70s textured swivel chair.

I was upset, but not because my parents were splitting up—I had no real concept of what that actually meant. I was upset because I was about to start kindergarten, and she said we were moving to LaMoure, North Dakota (population of about nine hundred). Buses only ran for rural kids, not town kids, meaning I wouldn't be riding the school bus to kindergarten.

This was devastating news. My older brother and two sisters had been riding the bus to school, and I desperately wanted my siblings to like me and believed that if I rode the bus with them, they would see me as an equal. Then maybe we would have built a strong, loving bond together as siblings. We would have shared laughs and forged unbreakable connections on that thirty-minute bus ride to school. They would have their friends over and ask me to play with them too. I would enthusiastically shout: *Yes, I'd love to.* We'd all smile, laugh, and adventure off having a jolly, feel-good time. Yes, that is how I dreamed it would go.

But it didn't.

Not only was I upset about not riding the bus, but I loved our farm—I still love our farm—and didn't want to leave it. My dad lived there for quite a few years after the divorce, so we often got to go visit. We had a nice-sized white house with a red roof that sat nearly a mile back from the main road. The house was never finished, but we lived there regardless. The open, main living space was finished so most of the activities took place in that area. There was an upper-level family room, but it never got proper flooring or drywall to cover the studs. It was just the bare, wooden bones with an oversized, beautiful, three-pane window facing towards the main road. We'd watch for the rare car to turn down our driveway or try to spot our cats and dog roaming around. This unfinished part of the house became our play and storage area. It had an upstairs loft—again, unfinished—where for fun we'd go through our grandparents' old war trunks. The loft's floor was loose plywood placed over the floor studs, so you had to watch your step; otherwise, you could break through. I would like to think my quick reflexes came from learning to safely navigate across that makeshift floor to the trunks of treasures and mysteries of that unfinished loft.

My favorite part of our farm was the carpet in our kitchen and dining room. It was dingy yellow adorned with colorful food words such as pepper, onion, and chicken. My sister Pam and I created a game where we would toss a small trinket on the carpet, and whichever word it landed on, we could only touch that word and try to cross the entire room.

The farm sat on about ninety acres consisting of pastures,

rolling hills, a rock pit, two barns, a Quonset hut, and a chicken coop. Bone Hill Creek ran a beautiful C-shape hug around us. Pam and I loved going down there and walking along the bank, exploring with our dog, Buster—a white cockapoo furball. We had other dogs, but he is the one I remember most.

We had plenty of farm animals growing up. I remember Grandpa Larry telling me we were raising horses to sell to the glue factory. I don't remember a lot about Grandpa Larry, but I'd like to assume he had a similar sense of humor to my dad's, where the horses were not indeed doomed to become school supplies. We also had pigs and cows in the barn down along the river bend. In order to get to the best fishing and swimming spot at the river, you had to walk along the fence between the two pastures and the barn area. I always envisioned the cows lowering their heads and charging us. We'd have to use our fishing poles as lances to fight off the charging heifers, but by some magical force, the cows seemed undisturbed by our presence.

Reaching the river was worth every worst-case scenario playing out in my imagination. That spot on Bone Hill Creek was perfect. It was on a bend, deep and wide, perfect for fishing and swimming. Just after the bend were some rippling rapids that offered the only way across. A steep, grassy slope was on the opposite side. You could usually see a few red and white bobbers snagged in the far bushes from casts that were a little too hard. If we wanted to retrieve our snagged bobbers we would have to follow a cow trail—watching for cow-pies—to reach the shallow rapids and slip our way across. Then we would have to maneuver like mountain goats on the steep incline of the hill to reach the bushes by the bank. But we were lazy people, so we'd usually just cut the line and restring a new bobber. Still to this day, bobbers are likely strung about the bushes on the bend.

It was a peaceful place, and I still go there via my meditations. Even though in reality it's now just a plowed-over field. The barn is gone, the cow-pies long ago tilled into the soil. In my meditations, though, I go back to the beautiful bend in the creek and smell the long grass of the pasture, which only pleases the senses of a farm kid. I learned to fish and swim there. I will always go back there.

What I did not love about our farm was *the forty*. This was a field that was set back behind the farm. To get to it, you had to cross over a culvert on a rinky-dink, makeshift, gravel bridge that was just wide enough to get a combine over. Even that required perfect alignment. You could easily imagine the three billy goats Gruff trip-trapping over the culvert to reach the field that wasn't full of grass; it was usually full of sunflowers.

Do you realize how tall sunflowers can grow? Up to sixteen feet. Imagine two Christmas trees stacked one on top of the other. Once when I was about seven, my entire family was all up at the forty, and I got lost. I couldn't find my way out and started crying. Everyone kept shouting at me to walk in a straight line, but then I would hear a noise and turn that direction. I'm sure it was only a few minutes, but it felt like hours and was terrifying. I was eventually saved by my dad holding up our cat, Blackington, just high enough over the yellow tops so I could see. I suspect seeing Blackington as a shiny, ebony beacon of safety was when my love of cats started. Once found, my other family members greeted me with frustrated laughs and annoyance. No loving embraces of concern or acceptance that I desperately wanted.

My dad, even though he was my savior from the forty, was not always the savior, but the provocateur. One day all of us kids

9

were riding in the bucket of a payloader,[1] and he headed up to the forty. As we crossed the culvert, he stopped and began to swing the bucket of the payloader back and forth.

Holy Shit! He's going to dump us all off the bridge!

I started screaming and crying. Everyone was telling me to calm down, but convinced he was going to dump us all out, and we were going to die, I couldn't. He'd run back to Mom and say: *Ha-ha. Finally got rid of those kids, hun. We can live a happy, peaceful life now.*

Clearly seeing my distress—or more likely alarmed that my screams might alert the neighbors five miles in any direction—he stopped his homicidal endeavor and put us safely back on the ground.

Trying to be cool so my siblings liked and accepted me was not going well. The need for social acceptance begins with fitting in with our families. If only I had been able to ride that damn school bus.

---

[1] Clearly rural life was different than city life in the late '80s, so please relax, helicopter parents; we all survived. This is what you do on farms.

3

Family Feelings

Maybe that was it. My mom couldn't handle my dad trying to murder her children by dumping us out of the payloader over a culvert. I also remember being thrown into the creek to "learn" how to swim. Both were plausible reasons for the divorce. But if I had to guess, it was probably because my dad might be the most frustrating person ever to have a conversation with. He can't answer a question to save his life. Literally.

My dad's health had recently declined. My siblings and I were guessing cancer since we knew he'd had some cysts removed, but he wouldn't tell us more than that. So we all got together to get a straight answer. He spent exactly thirty-eight minutes—I know this because I recorded it—telling us a story about his tracheotomy. Here's how just a bit of that conversation went.

"Dad, is it cancer?"

"Well, they know what they are doing."

"Dad, that's not an answer. We need to know."

"Well some of it could have been, not all of them, but you know how it goes."

"We don't. Can you at least tell us if you have a will written

11

down? We will need to know what you want done when that time comes."

"Well, Rita [his sister] knows what to do."

"Ok, so Rita is in charge?"

"Hell, no."

Ugh. I get it, Mom.

I am thankful that text messaging hadn't been invented yet when my parents were in high school. I probably would not exist. My dad's text messages are so cryptic, my mom would have never been able to know if he was asking her on a date or not.

I recently called him, and he didn't answer. I received this text in response:

> *Guess u called wrong dad,*
> *or tomorrow is like sign in*
> *bar,...... free beer tomorrow*
> *but it's.....still tomorrow?*

My dad has only hugged me once in my life that I remember, which was right before I deployed to Iraq. His Christmas gifts were mostly Mills Fleet Farm sliced orange candies along with inflatable float toys or a random squeaky toy. I've lived in the Twin Cities since 2005, and he has never once come to visit. He didn't even make it to my wedding.

Despite all that, I know he loves me.

Please don't think how awful and horrible he is. He's not. He did the best he could. Growing up in Dickey, we were taught to mind our own business. He was never able to see beyond what he knew. I'm not mad at him, so you shouldn't be either. He loves us. He loves his grandkids. He's an amazing grandpa. Our kids love going to Grandpa Jim's. They get to watch TV—outside, on the front steps. He's frustrating but not horrible. He expresses love, just not like a normal dad. Normal dads give hugs; he gives us potatoes.

Yes, to express his love he gives us regular ol' potatoes from the garden—even purple ones on occasion, which I really appreciate. I was eating purple potatoes before it was cool. Real love from Dad, though—deep, meaningful love—comes from frozen potatoes. Most people call them French fries, but not Jim. These are not your fancy Ore-Ida's classic cut. No, no, no. These come in a twenty-five-pound box of five, five-pound, unmarked brown bags fresh from the factory in Jimtown, which everyone else knows by its actual name, Jamestown.

If you have spent more than two minutes talking with my dad, you've talked potatoes. Before every trip to visit my dad, we are highly encouraged to bring a cooler, along with newspaper and plastic, to properly carry his frozen love offerings back home. During one particular trip my sister Amanda and I were getting ready to leave. My dad had just filled his two large deep freezers with frozen potatoes ... well, with what room he could. There were still plenty of Cool Whip containers, at least fifteen years old, sealed with worn masking tape, faded ink warning what frost-bitten meal was inside.

We had to break down the potatoes into style of fry and figure out how much weight he had of each, spending twenty minutes doing some math equation I hadn't attempted since high school. I know—why didn't we just count the bags? Clearly, reader, you don't know Jim. Trust me, we tried. In the end we had to determine how many would fit in everyone's freezers back at home.

"How big is your freezer at home?"

"I don't know; it's a pull-out drawer under my fridge."

"What do you mean you don't know how big your freezer is? Everyone knows what size freezer they have. And why don't you have a deep freeze? Everyone has a deep freeze."

"No, they don't, Dad. I live in a city, four minutes from a grocery store."

This is about as deep and intense of a conversation you'll ever have with my dad. We don't share feelings; we share potatoes.

Most of this don't-bother-anyone, mind-your-own mindset comes from my grandma. She was a wonderful, laid-back woman who let me brush her grey curls as a child. She canned the most delicious food and made the best strawberry rhubarb sauce. She never missed her programs: *Lawrence Welk* and *Jeopardy*. She enjoyed having a beer and slice a pizza for lunch—which she pronounced *peeza*. My grandma just wanted everyone to get along and not make a fuss. She passed the tradition of just letting things be and minding your own business to her children. My dad lived with my grandma after our farmhouse with the red roof deteriorated from neglect.

My dad isn't horrible, but he can be an ass. He has no patience. I hated when he yelled at Grandma for seemingly meaningless things. Grandma and I were heading to the town café just after a particularly awful exchange between her and my dad. As we climbed into her boat of a diesel car, I pushed the wait light and couldn't help but get angry for her.

"Grandma, don't let him talk to you like that. He's your son. He's living in your house. You can kick his ass out!"

She light-heartedly laughed, patted my knee, and said, "Oh, he's just your father."

She then pulled out her checkbook. "Well, let's get you your Christmas money now; you just never know if I'll make it until then."

It was still summer. She gave me twenty-five dollars more than the usual Christmas check. I think it was hush money.

On a side note, my Grandma made it until Christmas. In fact, she made it to many more Christmases. She started giving us our Christmas checks earlier and earlier each year saying she wouldn't make it until then. She lived well—at home—until she was ninety-two. She only spent the last couple months before her passing in a nursing home.

I'm happy I inherited the tall, lanky body build of the Schaubs and hopefully their longevity, but happier I didn't inherit their mindset. My brother Ken did not escape. He's very much like Dad. He's a Schaub in almost all traits. He can tell you such a story so he doesn't have to answer the question. He's a seasoned bullshitter. He's intelligent. He's very kind-hearted—his neighbor collapsed in his front yard, and Ken performed CPR until the ambulance came. Have no doubt; Ken has a big heart. But being a true Schaub, he's unable to see beyond what he knows, to acknowledge when he is wrong, or to accept responsibility. He's a dreamer, creative, and a big picture guy; he just can't see the details. And if you tell him this, you are wrong. And he embodies Dad to the fullest when he continually buys and hoards useless, broken things in hopes of fixing, selling, and making money on them.

My brother has made a lot of mistakes. I held fantasy expectations of what a big brother—not to mention husband, father, and military man—should be. Those expectations were never met. That is not his fault. I need to be respectful of who he

15

actually is and base my expectations around that. That is true for all relationships. Don't hold resentment or negative feelings towards someone because they didn't reach your expectations of what you thought they should be. Instead, set expectations based off who people are. We can't change people, so we need to change our perspective. Then people will change.

Amanda was born just after Ken, and they were two peas-in-a-pod. They ran around town together and caused some mischief. One of my mom's jobs was as a blackjack dealer for a local bar, so she was gone many nights. They took advantage of that.

Amanda and I have always been the closest among our siblings, and we are similar in that we have characteristics of both parents. No one would say: *You're just like your mother* or *You're just like your father* to us. We both seem to go for logic instead of feelings. She made some choices in her late teens that led to me having some beautiful nieces before most people become aunts. That was actually very fitting. Since Mom worked a lot, Amanda often had to be the caretaker in the family and did many of the mom things.

That also led her to the idea that she needed to make up for lost time. She could party and stay out until the sun came up. I have no idea how she did it.

She is one of the two people in this world that can talk me into doing shit that every bone in my body said is a bad idea.*Hey, let's stop at the Dickey bar and have one before we head back to LaMoure-*—and six hours later we'd stumble back into LaMoure. Clearly, this is an area where listening to my intuition needs improvement.

My sister Pam was closest in age to me. She's probably the

most thoughtful sibling and remembers events important to others. She will likely be the first to wish you a happy birthday or congratulate you on an anniversary. She's quiet compared to the rest of our loud family, but she gets in a good joke or two when she can.

We played together the most and shared a room at times but never grew especially close because from her perspective I'm the family favorite. And she's bitter about it. I don't know when that belief started, but I have a theory.

Shortly before I started writing this book, my dad recounted a story as the family sat around a rusty metal homemade fire pit next to the plowed potato field. Our seats were a variety of benches and chairs torn from junk cars. We roasted hotdogs on sticks, whittled down from the trees in Hobo Park ...

Let me stop your Google search right there. Hobo Park is the homemade park my dad created in his yard. It is nestled between the tree line and the potato field. It's where the town elders met up to drink beer and cook unsanitary meats. But I digress.

As we sipped on our Hamm's beer, he reminisced about the time it was just him and me in the house when I was about four or five. He needed something from the barn, which was a good quarter mile or so from the house, and he asked if I would be okay if he left for a bit.

Much like my dad, I am not a needy person, so I just looked at him and said, "Yup, I'm good."

His story reflects that in the eyes of my parents, I was self-efficient. And perhaps there was a subtext of chip-off-the-old-block pride in his remembrance. But Pam was born with some health issues, so naturally she required more care and time. From my perspective she got more love and attention than the rest of

17

us ever did. Yet she holds that against me. She struggles to see things from a different perspective. Everything happens *to* her, not *for* her. Sick kids are a lot of work—any parent can attest to this—so perhaps she feels their attention was a burden to them where my autonomy made me easier to take care of, therefore more favorable.

Whatever was bruising her psyche put a lot of stress on our relationship even into adulthood. For example, when my husband and I told the family we were ready to start a family, Pam and her husband had already been trying to get pregnant for three years. Since the Universe is always working for our highest good, it likely saw an opportunity for a lesson, and we both got pregnant about the same time. Her first then me nine weeks later. Still, she would see that my pregnancy happened to her.

I went to great lengths to acknowledge her first when I made the announcement that I was pregnant. I told my brother and sister-in-law Rachel before anyone else on my side of the family. Their first reaction was: *What will Pam do?* I told them to relax because I had a plan all set up.

The whole family was going to gather at a bowling alley to celebrate my niece Jacey's birthday. My task was to pick up the cake. So I had a second cake made that said, *Baby Berntson will have a new cousin to play with in October.* I was making it about her. Perfect, right? Wrong.

When the second cake box was opened, Pam was the first to see the inscription and immediately blurted, "You always have to steal my thunder, don't you?"

It crushed me. What should have been a fun, exciting moment was gone. Once people realized what was happening, they made an effort to be excited for me. Pam tried to play it off like she was teasing, but her bitterness was evident to everyone. I did my best to hide the tears, but I was devastated.

It was a big ugly mess. Since we don't talk about feelings in my family, I wrote her a letter. We ended up exchanging quite a few back and forth. I realized how deep-seated her resentment of me was. I also realized it wasn't me. It was her own demons and relationship with our parents that she was projecting onto me. We eventually talked it out and left the mess behind. We both said our peace.

Reflecting back on it now, I knew at the time it was a pivotal event, but didn't know why exactly until later when I finally understood the life lesson the Universe had smacked me over the head with: why did I think a cake could change my sister? It took me awhile to realize this and learn to accept what our relationship is. I continued to work on my perspective of it and what I could control. I moved on—or so I thought.

Apparently the hurt from that pregnancy fallout was just as deep-seated in me as her resentment of me. I didn't know this until I was fortunate enough to have a coaching call with Gabrielle Bernstein, a motivational speaker, life coach, author, and spiritual teacher. I absolutely love her and her books. During this coaching call I got to ask her for some advice. I told her I have a block to success. I fear that people will judge me for being successful. Success equals money, and where I grew up, anyone with money was deemed bad, selfish, or unworthy.

She asked a simple question. "What particular event comes to mind when you start to feel this judgment?"

Without hesitation I explained the situation with my sister. That surprised me since I didn't even consciously connect judgments of success with judgments from her.

Gabby then asked, "Why do you feel you have the right to feel that way?"

I didn't have an answer, which perplexed me. It seemed to please her since she explained that was a good thing and it would make it easier to let it go.

Since that and some other letting go exercises, I can more confidently say I have gotten closer to letting go of judgment. We have to be aware of judgment so we can recognize when it creeps in and handle it appropriately. Intuition doesn't work if we are in a state of judgment, either of ourselves or others. If you want to get better at recognizing your own judgment, pick up *Judgment Detox* by Gabby Bernstein. It's extremely helpful.

I love each and every one of my siblings. There is rarely a day that goes by when we don't communicate via Snapchat, messenger, or text. Each relationship is unique. We all get together as much as possible for camping, holidays, birthdays, or just any random reason. Have you ever seen the show *Chopped* on Food Network? It's where four chefs faceoff to prepare an appetizer, entrée, and dessert using mystery ingredients. After each round someone gets chopped. We do this as a family. We set up a pantry, have one of us create the mystery basket, appoint judges, and battle it out in the kitchen. It's one of our favorite pastimes.

Understanding our closest relationships through an unfiltered lens is an essential aspect of getting in tune with our intuition. These relationships don't have to be perfect and clean to be functional. They can be messy and downright ugly. That's fine; just knowing ourselves well enough and how we function within each relationship opens doors to our intuition.

When I found out I was pregnant, I intuitively sensed it was going to be a problem with Pam. Hell, my brother and sister-in-law knew it as well. But I ignored my intuition because it was easier to pretend I could create a wonderful, close, emotionally supportive bond between us with a cake. I blinded myself to reality. We will not be able to hear our intuition if we don't live in reality. If we are willing to accept the reality of our relationships, our intuition has the ability to strengthen our family bonds.

I didn't accept the reality of my relationship with Pam, so I wasn't listening to my intuition, and in the end we both were hurt. If I had accepted the reality of our relationship, if I had listened to my intuition, I would have prepared differently. She would have been upset regardless of what I did, but I could have told her separately from the family and given her time to process it on her own, let her work out her feelings about it first. But I decided to pretend a cake would take care of it.

From my perspective when growing up, my family sucked. I didn't fit in with them. Today I have a fun, awesome, closely-bonded family. Just a short time ago, we got together for a girls' weekend. We all had a blast—sang too much karaoke, drank way too much alcohol. We have all learned how to love and appreciate the uniqueness of our individual relationships—for the most part. No family is drama-free. Generally it happens around the card-table when there's a steady flow of beer. Someone will say something stupid. We have learned to either call them out or just side-glance our other siblings and silently cheers. The times when it goes too far, we take a smoke-break, potty-break, or drink-break—universal code words for: *Go calm the fuck down then come back.*

Usually any variety of "break" works and the family game continues. But it hasn't always been the case with my mom. For a long time she struggled with expressing herself freely. She would storm off in a huff about whatever, and we'd all look around and try to guess who or what had upset her. Half the time it was based on something she'd misheard or heard out of context that would then fester in her head until someone said something that released her pent-up anger or resentment, and she'd be gone. Reflecting on this now I think her emotional struggles stemmed from her blocking her own intuition.

My creative, extroverted personality comes from my mother. She's not one to shy away from saying what she thinks—good or bad. I don't say it like her, but my face usually gives me away. She cares deeply about everyone to a point of neglecting her own needs. Since she cares so deep, she tends to take everything to heart. Everything happens to her. She places a great deal of emotion, love, and value on material things that have never given her the like in return. When I was young, I gave her a glass cutting board for her birthday. She never used it, not even once. It sat on her kitchen counter for more than fifteen years. When my sisters and I helped her declutter, I asked "Mom, do you even use this cutting board?"

"No, it dulls the knives."

"Why do you have it then?"

"Well, you gave it to me."

My mom has struggled with mental health issues for as long as I can remember. When I was fourteen she drank too much and tried to kill herself. My sister Amanda stopped her, getting injured in the process. I went and lived with Amanda and her then-husband since mom had to go get some help. When Mom got back, she had a hard time adjusting. She felt very judged in our small town. She needed a change and asked if I would be fine moving to Valley City, a town about forty-five minutes north of LaMoure. After Pam took off for college in 2000, we boxed up and moved to a tiny apartment. We were both ready to reinvent ourselves and start new. We were both looking for acceptance.

All that seems so long ago, and I've seen some dramatic, amazing changes in my mom since then. My perspective on how to handle situations with my mother has changed. Just like my relationship with my siblings, learning to recognize the reality of our relationship and using my intuition to respond and react has been a major factor in strengthening our bond. I feel the changes are from my absurd and annoying positivity and from accessing my intuition. But also part comes from her own personal growth and letting go of things.

That glass cutting board is now dulling some thrift store shopper's knives as we speak.

4

Fitting in a Bra

There were plenty of signs that I didn't fit in the small-town lifestyle. My first kiss was with my friend Cody. Our friendship started because our sisters were good friends. We all just hung out, ate grilled cheese sandwiches at the Big Cone, and shot hoops beside their garage. One evening while playing basketball, our sisters dared us to kiss each other. I suspect his sister, Shawna, wanted to see if Cody would do it because his family had a sneaking suspicion he was gay. We later joked I turned him gay, but he was already there before the kiss. That's probably why we got along so well; both of us knew we didn't quite fit in.

Not only was Cody fun to be with, but his family was also one of the few in town with satellite television. The giant, gray dish in their front yard meant they could watch MTV. If you had cable, your only option to watch music videos was CMT (Country Music Television). Shania Twain's "Any Man of Mine" was one of the first music videos I remember. I watched that video over and over again, trying to learn how to be an attractive woman. This could definitely explain why I didn't get asked on dates and how my flamboyant gay best friend ended up my date to my high school prom.

As a tween I was able to escape LaMoure every once in a while and head over to Edgeley (pop. 550) where I'd run around with my friend Melissa. We would write plays that were usually about orphaned children—obviously, we were cool kids. There was a big pond that collected runoff from the intersecting roads behind her house. In the winter we would try to see how far we could get from the bank before the ice cracked too much. We'd usually come back with freezing wet pants up to our knees.

One time Melissa and I had just finished our ice cream from The Freeze, one of those old, walk-up ice cream shops that's stuck in time. The faded yellow-and-blue vintage sign watched as its neighboring business updated their signs, but the Freeze held strong. The wooden park bench in front usually had a local or two just chatting and gossiping. On that day though, some neighborhood boys were there. We probably started talking to them about how awesome our newest play was. When I spoke, they started whispering and looked at me with a weird expression on their faces.

Do I have something on my shirt? Are they not impressed by our playwright skills? Are they going to get their clubs? Whispers are bad! Oh crap!

"Where are you from?" ventured one of the whispering boys.

I immediately anticipated this was going to end in tears from being teased mercilessly about something. *Breathe.*

"Why?" I managed to ask.

"You sound funny. Are you from Australia or something?"

I responded with a nervous laugh, and Melissa started laughing too. Thankfully, she took charge and explained I was just from LaMoure and said they were dumb because they didn't know what Australians sounded like.

While I did once create a sweet diorama of the Great Barrier Reef in a shoebox, that was as close as I'd ever been to Down Under. However, I had a lisp. I had to spend three years staying in from recess multiple times a week to work with a speech teacher who—in true small-town fashion—was family: Grandma Schaub's niece, DeAnna. Apparently a recovering lisper sounds Australian. We hopped on our bikes and rode away, silently feeling victorious that we made it through with feelings intact and continued to see whether Annie would ever get adopted.

Funny enough, I don't remember being teased much about my lisp, which is likely me blocking out that part of my childhood. But I do remember getting teased over my clothing and family. We weren't particularly highly regarded in LaMoure. To support us four kids after the divorce, my mom worked in the bars a lot. My siblings tended to get in trouble and throw parties. Everyone in my family, besides my dad and me, smoked cigarettes. Because I was constantly around the stench, I was the smelly kid. It didn't help that because my mom worked so much, she didn't have time to enforce tidying up or bath time. *Schaub the slob* was a term I heard more than a few times.

On top of being the smelly bar family, we were poor too. I was watching television with my mom one evening when a commercial for a local car dealership came on. It said you could lease a new vehicle for around $100 a month. Our old family car was always breaking down.

I said, "Mom, that isn't a lot of money; maybe we can get a new car."

She snorted a disgruntled laugh and said something to the effect: *I can barely afford to feed you kids each month, let alone afford a new car.*

I remember feeling sad for my mom and our family. We couldn't afford food. I knew we were on food stamps. We often had unlabeled cans of food on our shelf, products from the food bank. This was no way to live. I didn't want to just survive. There had to be more than that. I made a promise to myself then that I would not live paycheck to paycheck when I grew up. I would be able to buy a car when I needed to. I would be able to buy food for the sake of enjoying it. *I will do more than just survive.*

But for the time being I still had to endure hand-me-downs. It wasn't so much that they were *gently used*; it was that my body type was quite the opposite of my sisters'. They were born Andersons—broad, strong, stocky, and of average height. I was born a Schaub—tall, skinny, lanky. Somehow that disparity was not one of my mother's concerns as she insisted I could fit into their clothes, leaving me an easy target for teasing, mocking, and ridicule. But somehow I didn't take most of the teasing personally.

I often thought: *What's wrong with these people?* and not: *What's wrong with me?* Most of the harassment was about material things and not about me personally. People wanted to attack and tease me because of my clothes? It just seemed absurd and illogical to me. Even at a young age, I was listening to my intuition without knowing it. I understood intuitively that bullies were stupid and just projecting their own issues.

A new policy at school prohibited students from wearing or possessing any items that advertised alcohol or tobacco began and it helped reduce some of the teasing about my hand-me-downs. My Marlboro duffle bag would no longer work for gym class and collecting all of those hard-earned cigarette UPC labels would no longer serve my wardrobe.

For as much of a relief as that was, it didn't address what bothered me the most—my mom's insistence that I wear my sisters' hand-me-down bras. When the time came for me to get some much needed support, she ordered my sisters to put all their old bras that didn't fit into the bathroom for me to try on. I remember looking down at the pile of stretched out, stringy, random-sized bras on the floor. Looking in the mirror I cupped my small chest, hoping my fairy godmother would pop in any time now to save me. Maybe turn the pile of bras into a Victoria's Secret store. But I didn't see any shiny, glittery fairy godmother orb coming in and knew I was doomed. I caved and put one on. I could wrap it nearly twice around my slender frame. I wanted to fit in, and these bras were not going to help.

I talked to my mom about my lack of support options, and she said we couldn't afford new clothes right now. So if I wanted to fit in a bra, it was up to me. I had already started getting babysitting jobs, so I knew I could make money. I even sold stuff out of magazines to try and earn money although my grandmas were usually my only buyers. Still, those ratty old bras were a lesson from the Universe. I suppose now I could say they were a gift from the Universe. Back then, though, it was just a pile of reality. That's when I realized I wasn't going to be able to rely on anyone else. If I needed something, I'd have to figure it out on my own.

While I could rationalize others' teasing, it wasn't always easy; there were times when words went straight into my young, impressionable soul. I found my fifth-grade diary awhile back. There were a lot of tear-stained pages that said the same thing: *Ashley is so mean. The next time she says something mean to me, I'm not going to be her friend anymore.*

Ashley is my second cousin who lived next to us in LaMoure.

We played a lot together, rode bikes to school every morning, found my cat Speed Bump together after we heard her crying on the way to school. Poor kitty was stuck under a bush. She was still there on our way home, so we pulled her out. When we brought her to the house, she snuggled right into my mom's sizable chest, and that was it. We had a new kitty. For the record I did not pick the name Speed Bump. My brother gets that glory.

Ashley and I won our Just Say No lock-in Lip-Sync Contest. Just Say No is pretty much the generic version of the DARE anti-drug campaign. I can still rock all the dance moves we practiced for hours whenever I hear "Ironic" by Alanis Morissette. We had wonderful times. Like any friendship of a tween, it had its ugly moments too.

Does anyone remember skorts, skirts with shorts underneath? They were cool for about two hot minutes. I had one a sweet black pair, either handed down or donated, I don't remember, but I was happy with it either way. I was going to be stylish instead of basic. I went over to Ashley's for our usual meet up and ride to school.

She came out the door, stood on top of the steps, gave me a once over, and announced, "Those are so ugly. You should just cut the skirt off."

I pretended she was the fashion-backward one and ignored her advice. Throughout the day she made sure the cool kids noticed and made fun of me. I get it now, she was just trying to be cool too. Who wants to be seen with the uncool kid? I never wore them again, even though I still defend the coolness of my skort. My daughter has a pair of black pants with a black sequin skirt over it. (Skants?) Those are cool. I mean she's four, but whatever.

Teachers also knew I didn't fit, and their conservative small-town views often squashed my creativity. For example, we all had to write a limerick, illustrated with a picture, to be displayed in the hallway like many of our projects were. I hung mine up proudly then started to head out for recess but was asked to stay behind. My teacher felt my limerick was inappropriate and had to be taken down. I don't remember it exactly, but it went somewhere along the lines of:

> *There once was a man named Bart.*
> *He ate a big ole' blueberry Pop-Tart*
> *He ate too many*
> *Got an ache in his belly*
> *And couldn't help but let out a loud fart.*

They didn't recognize the greatness that could have been.

I tried to fit in with the popular girls, which ended up with them being really mean to me. The mean girls liked to invite people like me over to one of their houses to hang out. Once I rolled up on my bike, they would start talking about some other kid in school.

Oh my gosh, isn't so-and-so so annoying?

Oh my gosh, she totally is. She can't even read out loud in class.

Then they'd stared at me, waiting.

Intuitively, all the alarms were ringing. *This sounds bad! So-and-so is a friend.* But they were the popular kids. I needed to fit in. I had no choice but to agree.

"Yeah, and she's so ugly too, right?"

An evil, pleased smile would stretch across their un-pimpled faces.

Weee-ooo! Weee-ooo! Danger, Will Robinson, Danger!

Then the lucky topic of conversation would leap out of the garage or appear from around the corner, turning my insides to shit. Every mean girl along with the hiding mark then made you feel terrible for saying such awful things about your friend.

Sometimes I was able to pull off the: *Oh, I knew you were there, I was just playing along* defense, but most of the time I rode home on my bike with tears streaking my cheeks, listening to the cruel laughter fade behind me.

When I'd finally had enough of being the victim of these games, I thought I'd try my hand at being mean. I wanted to be like everyone else, so maybe if I was mean to other people, they would like me, and I would start fitting in. My brain would function like the rest of my friends. I'd be cool, accepted, and finally happy.

I was given a chance to be mean when a new kid, Kimberly, moved into town. She had long, black hair and was clever, so of course she became a target. I had partnered up with my cousin Ashley on this mean train, and it didn't take long for Kimberly to have her fill of us. One day in biology we were learning about diseases and the microorganisms that make us sick. After the bell rang and we were leaving class, Kimberly handed us a drawing captioned *The two worst pathogens.* Ashley's name was above one and mine above the other.

We snatched the paper and went to the teacher, flashing the evidence of such cruelty. After what I think now in retrospect were some stifled smiles, she said would talk to Kim about it. I don't know if she ever did, but Kim did not get in trouble despite our physical proof. I was pissed. I wanted justice and revenge for all the times people were mean to me and never got in trouble. This was the opportunity. That old pile of stretched out bras had taught me a lesson I needed to apply here. This was a situation I would have to handle by myself.

We were in a crowded school hallway later that week. Kim and I bumped shoulders passing each other.

"Kim, you're such a bitch," I snarled at her.

Well, of course she went and told the teacher. Guess who had to spend a week inside from recess in the principal's office as punishment? That's right—me! With no evidence except her word, I ended up in trouble. I felt it was such an unjustified punishment. No other bully or mean girl ever got punished for picking on me, yet the one time I try it, I get in trouble. However, people walked by the office during my punishment and gave me a thumbs up. That helped me feel better. People were on my side. This was a chance to fit in. I was finally being accepted.

So why didn't it feel good? From the outside I seemed accepted socially. But internally I felt rejected by myself. I got what I thought I wanted and still felt awkward.

My social acceptance didn't last long. School pictures from then to freshmen year made sure there was always ammunition for people to use against me. I had earned enough money from babysitting to buy a new outfit for picture day. I picked out a super soft, green turtleneck sweater from Walmart. I did my hair in a cool half ponytail and used some of my sister's makeup trying to conceal my acne.

After I walked into school, it took all of three minutes for someone to say, "Did someone throw up on you? Your shirt looks like vomit."

Ugh. Kids are assholes. Don't let your kids be assholes.

5

Yeah, I'll do That

Speaking of assholes, my siblings often fell into that category. Ken and Amanda were closest in age, so they partnered up against Pam and me. They used my need of acceptance against me.

We had a sock box growing up. For those of you from non-lazy families, a sock box is where you throw all the socks—unmatched—into a grocery store cardboard box after laundry. It was then up to the wearer to find a matching pair. I often wore two different socks and tried to play it off as a fashion statement. But as you can probably guess, it didn't work. On a side note, I'm annoyed that it's a thing kids do now. I promise you it started because some popular kid had a sock box at home.

Anyway, Ken and Amanda thought it would be funny to tie both Pam and me up using socks. This was legit cow-roping style tied up. There was actual fear of my hands turning purple and falling off. I could not express that concern since our mouths were gagged with socks. They eventually removed the gags after we promised not to scream. We were then forced to bob for apples to be set free. This was hilarious to them, terrifying for us.

Have you ever bobbed for apples? It's incredibly difficult with the full use of legs and hands, let alone with sock locks around them. I imagined Mom coming home and finding us dead, with our heads in the water, our legs up in the air with socks holding them together. How would they explain this in our obituaries for the *LaMoure Chronicle*?

Another a-hole thing my siblings did was use me as a guinea pig. My grandma lived at the edge of Dickey on a good chunk of land with beautiful rolling hills of cow pastures and fields. These were literally the best sledding hills you could hope for growing up. There were some rocks, small trees, bushes, and cow pies, but the slopes were perfect. Just as we had to walk through the cow pastures to go fishing, we had to walk through the cow pastures to reach the hills.

All of us would trudge through the freshly fallen snow, making sure the cows were occupied over at the salt lick or hay. These cows were more vicious than the ones at our farm. If they charged, no plastic sled was going to save us. Once we had the all clear, we would head to the fenced path they would open so the cattle could go up the hills and graze in the summer. We would climb the hill and find what we thought was the perfect route to sled.

It took me a few years to learn something of great value. I was often given the "privilege" of doing the first pass. *Okay, Becky; you get the exciting chance to go first.* They were so enthusiastic. They were being so kind. Me, the baby of the family, getting to do something first.

Hell, yeah; I'll go down first!

It took me a while to figure out that they sent me down first to see if any rocks, trees, shrubs, or cliffs were in the way. Somehow I managed to survive most runs unscathed. One time I did manage to find a huge cliff that launched me right off the sled. As I landed I thought for sure I'd broken every bone in my body—or at least my butt. Thankfully, I walked away unbroken.

For many years I did anything they asked of me. They knew I would, knew I was eager to please them. That eagerness put my life at risk on more than one occasion. It would always start the same way.

"Hey, Becky Jo; you want to join us?"

You want to spend time with me? Before even knowing what we were doing, I always shouted, "Yes!"

One time someone had the great idea to use the icy alley behind our house as a sled track. Seemed legit. Then they insisted that I be the first one to ride in the sled—obviously because I was so cool. The sled was attached to the back bumper of our Oldsmobile by a long rope. I climbed on the sled all giddy as my smiling siblings peered down at me. They looked so happy that I was hanging out with them. Ken got into the car and took off. It was a slight jerk at first, but then it was super fun, like sledding down a hill but better—until he slammed on the brakes at the end of the alley.

The car stopped. I didn't.

Not having any braking mechanism, I continued at the same rate as before—fun feelings gone. Instinctively I raised my arms to shield my face and caught the bumper, which stopped me from barreling under the car and getting mangled into oblivion. Another fun obituary for the *Chronicle* to write.

I did escape actual physical harm in most of those misadventures until one particular evening.

"Hey, Becky; we're throwing a party tonight. You're not allowed to come out."

My room was next to the living room. I had to endure the party regardless of whether I was invited or not. At one point I got hungry and wanted a snack. I hoped that if I just walked straight to the kitchen, it would be fine. I had to cross the open living and dining room but told myself they were all drunk, and no one would notice me, even though intuitively I knew it would not work like that, but my stomach's cravings trumped my good sense.

I walked out at literally the exact worst time, just as one partygoer decided to battle-axe toss a Marks-A-Lot Jumbo marker from the dining room to the living room. It was a direct hit to my blonde, teen-bop head. The loud shriek that exploded from my lungs froze the drunkards, whose eyes darted towards the source of the high pitched scream.

As I took my hand off my throbbing head, I saw more blood than I was ready for. I didn't quite grasp what had actually hit me, but once I realized it was a marker, I assumed it must have had a razor blade taped to it. I still can't understand how it cut me like it did. Ken quickly ushered me into the bathroom and tried to doctor me up.

"Don't tell Mom," he kept drunkenly repeating.

He set down his beer and dug out the isopropanol alcohol as I sat on the toilet crying. It took some convincing and false promises before I let him get near my cut with the alcohol. I assumed the alcohol would make it hurt more and burn. He finally got me to settle down and was able to clean it up—a fine example of how his bullshitting ability is a good thing—then he ushered me back to my room. The next time, I remembered to bring snacks to my room before the party started.

There were countless other examples of seeking love and acceptance from my siblings. Pam and I would get haircuts at the same time. She once got an awesome bowl cut with the underside shaved while I kept my long hair and just had my ends trimmed.

Everyone in school commented on her hair, but nobody noticed mine. I wanted to be noticed too. Obviously it was my flowing, blonde hair that was the problem. I somehow convinced my mom to take me back that week and got the same sweet bowl haircut.

The constant need to be liked by my siblings came to an abrupt halt when I was twelve. At the end of each school year, the sixth graders were invited to join the junior high and high schoolers at the school dance as a way to welcome them to their upcoming big kid school days. I couldn't wait. I loved dancing. I was pumped all year and practiced countless hours of dancing. I had all the moves to "Cotton Eye Joe" down and all the words to "I Like It, I Love It" by Tim McGraw. This was it. This was going to be my break. I would become popular and fit in.

When the date was officially announced for the end of the year dance, I told my siblings how excited I was. They informed me that it was uncool to go to dances. Nobody went to them, and if they did, they aren't people you'd want to be seen with.

That crushed my dreams. I thought this would be my moment. But I trusted them. They were family, so I listened to their advice. I told my friends I wasn't going because it was uncool and whatever other lame excuses I could come up with. I stayed home. My brother and sisters were just watching out for my best interest, right?

The next day I woke up a bit disappointed but felt like I had stood my ground and was headed into the cool phase of school. Later that day, I talked to my friends who told me about how much fun they had dancing all night and dancing with each other and even with boys.

Trying to hide my jealousy, I played the cool card. "Well, my brother and sister said dances are lame, and people don't go."

Looking confused, one of my friends responded, "What are you talking about? They were there too. Everyone was."

They went to the dance? How could they? Those assholes lied to me so they wouldn't have their uncool sister with them. I heard some dial turn in my head. All of sudden my intuitive voice became clear. Something clicked into place. A part of my personality was set in. The old ratty bra life lesson emerged again. *I don't need them. I can figure this out on my own. I can do life myself.* That's when I decided I no longer cared to please them. My need to be accepted by them had blocked my intuition. I should have gone to the dance. I was going to do things for myself. I didn't want to be like them anymore. They were the uncool ones now, not me. Screw those guys.

A new girl moved to town that summer. Holly. That whole mean girl act hadn't worked out well for me with the last new girl. This time, with my new-found independence and attitude, I decided to follow my intuition and be true to myself and befriend her. We became very good friends. Now that I no longer sought or needed my family's acceptance, I actually found a circle of really good friends. We were all odd ducks. A closet homosexual, a home-schooler, a do-gooder, a quiet introvert, and a daughter of the principal.

Letting my need of family acceptance go was a first step toward my intuition. Only after letting go did things start to fall into place. Part of that is just growing up and maturing, but if we allowed our intuition to help us along the way, we could learn to manage our lives better. We would experience what really matters most—self acceptance.

I participated in dance and track and field and also played

basketball for one year. I was tall with gangly arms, so everyone naturally thought I would be an ideal basketball player. The school had gotten new uniforms a few years earlier. My class of forty-seven people—the second biggest in the school—had more players than upgraded uniforms. So rather than cut anyone, three members of the team were issued the old uniforms, which were faded yellow with age. They said it was random, but I couldn't help but notice that the three people that got them were the three who were only in the game for the last couple of minutes.

But I had some sweet moments in those few minutes of playing time. I made the classic take-off-the-wrong-way-down-the-court move. One time I raced down the court full speed to assume my defensive position with my gangly, foul-creating arms. While running I glanced over my shoulder to see where the ball was. When I turned back I saw a flash of white and black stripes before going crashing into the big-bellied referee. Who happened to be the principal. Who happened to be one of my best friends dad. Not impressed with my skills yet? I lost a contact lens during a game once. I played most of my few minutes of fame half blind. It actually worked out because somehow I magically made a few shots. My coach suggested I wear only one lens for the rest of the season.

No, basketball was not for me. Since I loved to dance, I joined the school dance team instead. I had rhythm and was a quick learner. The structured and synchronized movements of dance appealed to my fairly unstructured home life. Practices were tough but I hardly missed them. One year as the state dance competition neared, I was stretching during our practice, working on my splits and finally got them down. I went over to show my friend Mary. But as I went into my splits, I heard an extremely loud pop, followed by incredible pain. I immediately grabbed my leg and started crying. Here's a problem: my laugh and my cry sound very much the same in that you don't really hear either. I'm a creepy silent laugher and crier. So Mary initially thought I was laughing before she understood what had happened. Long story short, I tore some muscle in my leg. My team had to re-choreograph their entire state routine in less than a week, as I hobbled around on crutches.

When track and field season came around the following spring, I was convinced I wouldn't be able to run because of my previous leg injury, so I threw things. I did shotput and discus. I wasn't bad but wasn't really good either. During one meet a relay team was short a runner, and I was the only sub available because everyone else had participated in four events already, which was the max you could do.

Somehow Mr. Toppen, our science teacher/track coach, convinced me to run a leg of the race. Mr. Toppen was an odd, goofy guy. He was new to LaMoure. An outsider is always odd. It wasn't popular to like him, so I pretended I didn't, but I actually enjoyed his classes. I seemed to like the odd folks. Our intuition often leads us to those of similar energies.

Something strange happened when I ran that race. I did really well. I was faster than everyone else on the relay team. It was something I was actually good at. People came up genuinely pleased—perhaps surprised—that I did so well and said nice things to me. That was a new experience for me. Up to then nobody had ever given me any attention for being good at anything. After that Mr. Toppen threw me into every sprinting race he could—the 400, 200, and 100-meter dash along with relay races. It was now my life. I was a runner. I loved it. Sadly, he later left for a new teaching job and moved out of town, and we got a new coach.

I couldn't afford real track spikes. I just had regular tennis shoes for my first couple of races. One of the sprinting coaches realized this and gave me a pair to use. That was the first time someone reached out to help me. Someone thought I was worth helping. They saw I could be something more. I felt if someone was going to be generous to me, I should make the most of it. I didn't want them to regret helping me, so I pushed a little harder than I ever had before.

Little gestures like that are sometimes all it takes to convince kids they are capable of more than they know. If you can be that person for a kid, the payoff will be more than you can imagine. Be that person, even if just once. That simple act of kindness literally set the standard for the work ethic I have carried with me since.

My track career in LaMoure didn't last long. The following summer, my mom and I moved to Valley City. My LaMoure Loboe days were over. I was starting my sophomore year as a Valley City Hi-Liner.

This is it, I thought. *Here is a chance for me to fit in. I can re-invent myself or possibly even be myself. I can be accepted.*

6

Valley Girl

I managed to make friends fairly quickly in Valley City. On the first day of my sophomore year, I wore an Old Navy blue tank top and khaki shorts. I wanted to say *I know name brand stuff*, but I couldn't afford much, so Old Navy would have to do. It apparently paid off as the group of girls I went up to seemed to take me in.

I'm grateful I worked up the courage to approach Lindsey, Stephanie, and Al as they stood next to the lockers. I said something to the effect: *Hi, it's my first day. I'm a sophomore, and I feel weird standing alone.*

They responded: *Oh! We thought you were a freshman.*

We were able to build a friendship off the shared view of how stupid and immature freshmen were. They continued to be my best friends for the rest of high school, and I keep in contact with a couple of them. After I went to Iraq and moved to Minneapolis-St. Paul, we lost some of what we'd had in common. But they were invaluable to me and taught me so much about life outside of a small town. I could have walked up to any group of kids that first day of school, but I picked them. Thank you, Universe.

I could have walked up to the stoner kids. That would have

been interesting. One thing I learned quickly about the big city (by North Dakota standards) was that drugs were everywhere. I thought this kid Kenny was hot. I asked my new friends about him. They quickly warned me that he was a hardcore stoner kid. I was taken aback. Sorry, Kenny; drugs are not cool.

I had no idea people in my part of the world did drugs. I thought just city kids smoked weed because that's what TV told me. I did learn much later in life that there had been plenty of times when paraphernalia was around. Didn't everyone get the message, *Just Say No?* I was just naive and sheltered from all of it. We didn't have satellite TV. The twenty channels we received aired local news, Lawrence Welk, soap operas, and country music—not a whole lot of cultural diversity.

When you're from a small town, it can be hard to grasp how the rest of the world functions. We're busy watching out for villager mob attacks. Also, when I grew up, most of us didn't have the internet. (Jeez, I feel old saying that.) Trust me; I tried to figure out how to make the fancy AOL disk with dial-up work without a credit card on multiple occasions.

Most people in a rural communities live in their own small-town world and generally develop the us vs. them mentality. We go along with whatever everyone tells us because it's the path of least resistance. Since nobody wants to become a saber-toothed tiger's lunch, the us vs. them mindset predominates, and it can be seen in politics, war, and various other group settings. It's just not an issue with small towns. My small hometown simply makes it obviously observable.

My nineteen-year-old niece from North Dakota recently came to visit with a friend from Georgia. She said to her friend, "You have entered the land of liberals."

43

I asked, "Do you even know what being a liberal means?"

She didn't, so she replied, "I don't want to."

That prime example of small-town mentality literally pained me.

If you are not part of the *us*, then you are the *them*. It is easier to be part of the us.

In LaMoure an us vs. them mindset is also applied to social classes in town. I had plenty of so-called friends tell me they couldn't hang out with me because of my family life dynamics.

Your mom works in a bar, and your family drinks and smokes, so my mom says you can't come over.

When we moved to Valley City, my new friends didn't do that to me. They were always kind and never seemed to care that my mom and I were poor. They never flinched if I couldn't afford to do something. They didn't look around in disgust or seem to be bothered by hanging out in our tiny, seven-hundred-square-foot apartment.

It did bother one of my friend's dad. We were able to leave the school campus for lunch hour, a privilege given to seniors. We often went to Steph's house, made turkey sandwiches, and had chips with cheesy jalapeño dip. We left school during lunch for no other reason than we simply could. One particular day I overheard a conversation between Steph and her dad after he pulled her aside. He told her she shouldn't bring me over for lunch anymore because I was just using her for food since I came from a poor, single-parent home.

Steph's mom worked at the school, so I'm sure she knew we got food assistance from the state to pay for my school lunches. Steph told her dad he was being ridiculous, and we left right after. I stopped going for a while even though she assured me it was fine. But her father had made comments a few other times indicating he didn't like his daughter hanging out with someone from a lower class. It still bothered me.

He was one of those people I put on my imaginary list that when I made it, I'd come back and say: *Fuck you and your judgmental privileged ass!*

But here's the deal; I'm only a mean person in my head. In reality it never comes out that way. I've imagined all sorts of scenarios where I tell people off. I prepare for an epic confrontation full of witty comments and zingers. Then when the time comes to have that conversation, I'm super nice. It's not that I'm being fake. I just don't believe in being an asshole. Also, during my preparations I generally work out any anger or resentment. It's all released before the actual conversation happens. And it's all good. How many times have you imagined a conversation and it went as you planned? Yeah, that's what I thought—zero. It never works out as planned. What we think is never the reality.

Years after high school I ended up sitting next to them at a mutual friend's wedding. Steph's mom is the sweetest mom you'd ever meet. I really enjoyed catching up with her since Steph wasn't able to attend the wedding. I told her about my job working full-time in the military and that I just bought a house. They were genuinely happy and proud of me. Someone's genuine happiness always feels better than being an asshole.

My other friend Allison, her dad, Scott, is quite the opposite of Steph's. Every year their family took a trip to Mexico. Each of their kids got to pick a friend to bring along. Allison asked if I could go and said her parents would pay for the plane ticket, so I just had to cover expenses. Although I had zero dollars and I had never traveled further than Nebraska, I was determined to make this Mexico trip happen. But I was working two jobs already and had to help my mom out with the bills so I had to talk to my Grandma about getting some money to go. She cashed in my savings bond early and was able to get me enough to be able to go. I was excited and proud that I figured out a way to make it work. *Thank you, ratty old bras.*

Before our flight we stopped at a KFC. I went up to the counter, ordered, and got my money out.

Scott stopped me. "I got it."

"No, I got money from my Grandma—"

He interrupted and said with a bit more forcefulness, "I got it."

I stepped back and waited for the others to order. He stood next to me and carefully said, "You're not paying for anything on this trip, do you understand?"

I wanted to be embarrassed, I wanted to stand my ground and say I had figured it out. I wanted to say I was fine. But for some reason, I couldn't. The way he said it, I wasn't able to feel embarrassed. He didn't have an ounce of judgment or resentment in his voice. It was just a sense of: *I'll take care of you.*

That was new. Only a used pair of track spikes had given me that sense before. I just figured I would always take care of things myself. That was the first crack in my ratty bra mentality. It's not that my parents didn't take care of me. They just literally and physically couldn't the way they wanted to. I never expected someone outside of my family to take care of me—or want to. Especially if they didn't have to. They accepted me as is.

I'm still very best friends with Al and her family. After high school and on trips back to Valley City, I'd often ask her how I could ever repay her parents for all the things they had done for me. How do you repay people who can literally buy anything they would ever want or need? One year I was able to figure that out.

After a few beers at the Captain's Pub and some prodding, I learned that Scott wanted to go down to Boomer's Corner Keg. He had never been there. Boomer's is a biker bar, so most people don't stroll in and expect to be greeted with open arms. You need an in. Well, my mom and family hung out with the biker crowd. I'm welcomed with warm hugs there.

So I said, "Well, let's go to Boomers!"

The only condition was they had to order a special *"A"* beer. It's not the beer that's special. It's that you're drinking out of a frosty, thirty-six-ounce mug with etched boobies on it. Boomer himself takes the pictures then etches them on. I personally don't think a four dollar, frosty beer with boobs on the mug in a biker bar equals a trip to Mexico, but it was something I could happily provide.

Even though my parents' lifestyle was drastically different from my friend's parents, our friendships and high school life were very similar. I think it boils down to something simple; all of us were cash-poor high schoolers. I had no choice to grow up anything but poor. While my friends grew up with plenty of money in their families, their parents did right by them and didn't give in to their needs and wants. They were expected to work. We all drove old hand-me-down cars. I can't tell you how many times we'd pull up to Corner Convenience in Lindsey's blue Dodge Neon or Steph's green Taurus and say: *Five dollars, please.* The CC as we called it was the only full-service gas station with an attendant that would fill the tank for you. They would give us that evil glare after we handed them our five-dollars, often in change, and we would slowly roll up the window with exaggerated, embarrassed smiles on our faces.

7

Big Wheel Beckster

Besides cruising main street with my new Valley friends, I did the same extracurricular activities: dance team and track. But not basketball. Ugh, never again. On the first day of school, one of the reasons my friends thought I was a freshman was the school actually put me in freshman level classes. I finally got in the right classes after lunch, starting with biology. As I made my way to the third floor where the science classrooms were located, I double checked my new schedule and noticed my teacher's name was Mr. Randy Toppen.

I paused on the stairs. *He won't remember me, right? How will I be able to reinvent myself if someone here knows me?* I shook it off and finished the climb. I didn't listen to that little intuitive buzz in my ear. I convinced myself it would all be okay.

The bell rang as I walked into the classroom. Everyone was already there. I had to let Mr. Toppen know about my messed up schedule since I wouldn't be on his roster. I approached cautiously.

"Hi…" He looked up at me, and I quickly continued. "My schedule was messed up, so I'm probably not on your attendance sheet."

A huge smile of recognition spread across his face. "Big Wheel Beckster, is that you?"

I hear the once chatty class go silent behind me. *Fuck.* I didn't know how to respond. *How I do play this?*

"Yes, Mr. Toppen, it's me." *Dammit.* So clever.

I can't remember if he went on to explain his nickname for me. Did he announce to the class that he called me Big Wheel Beckster because I was a fast and amazing sprinter? Or was it left awkwardly to brew in everyone's mind? I have tricked my mind into remembering the former, but it is much more likely the latter.

While sitting in one of my classes the next day an older guy walked in. He had salt and pepper hair with dark eyes that his big-framed glasses didn't hide. His blue windbreaker crinkled as he strolled up to the teacher. I couldn't hear exactly but thought I heard him say my name. The teacher confirmed that suspicion by pointing in my direction. He looked in my direction with a big goofy grin and waved at me to go out into the hall. I followed him out even though I was confused and had no idea who he was. That was my introduction to Mr. Bill Jansen, the track team's giddy and excited head coach.

Mr. Big Mouth Toppenster had talked about me with Mr. Jansen—everybody called him Mr. J—who wanted me to join their cross-country team. I assured him that I would run track in the spring, but 2.1 miles seemed extreme; I'd never run more than a 400-meter dash. Even so, there was something about him that I felt very comfortable with, and I finally said yes.

Mr. J was one of those guys you couldn't help but love. It's hard to put into words the way he could make you feel. He pushed you with crazy hard workouts where all you could think about was whether puking or passing out was the better option to get a break. He gave every athlete a color-coded 3-ring binder with all of their stats and information from all of the meets. It had history, records, and stats from his entire coaching career to help and inform and inspire us.

Looking back I can see I was a good athlete, but I didn't apply myself as much as I should have, could have. My work ethic often collided with the desire for acceptance. I listened to the peer pressure instead of my own intuition and those who knew I was better than what I was doing. Therefore, I wasn't really good, but I did enjoy cross-country running and the camaraderie of the team. After every meet held in Jamestown, we always stopped at the Golden Fork Buffet, per Mr. J's rules.

Because of my poor mindset, I didn't run cross-country my senior year. They had a rule that if you ran cross-country, you could not play in the powder-puff football game against the junior class team. I wanted to play that football game, so I skipped an entire season of cross-country for a one-night game. I was so dumb.
   He didn't see that though. Mr. J tried relentlessly to get me to go out again, but I didn't listen. Looking back, it's one of my few regrets. I don't have many. I don't necessarily believe everything happens for a reason. I do believe there are lessons—or as Gabby Bernstein calls them, assignments in life—to learn. In high school I was given an assignment to push beyond myself. To trust my intuition. To listen to people that I respected and loved. I apparently wasn't ready to learn that lesson. To be fair, most teenagers aren't. God bless all teachers, coaches, and parents who try talking logic and reason to high schoolers to no avail. Your voices and concern matter. Even though it may not be understood

at the moment, the lessons and assignments will still be there later. Although I didn't do cross-country my senior year, I still ran track. It was not my best year performance-wise. I had been a much better, faster runner my junior year. However, Mr. J believed in me more than I ever believed in myself. He believed in me more than anyone I'd known before. He constantly pushed me out of my comfort zone. During one of our track meets, he put me in back-to-back races.

"I can't run a 400 meter-relay, then the 200-meter dash right after the mile. You're crazy!"

His dark eyes lit up behind his glasses. With his big goofy grin, he said, "I wouldn't have signed you up if I didn't think you could do it."

I huffed away in a fit, still convinced he was crazy. I went down to the field and began my warm-ups. I was mad and frustrated, not thinking I would survive the day. *Mr. J has lost his damn mind.*

I did the races. I didn't win. Not even close, but I did them. Mr. J just smiled.

I blamed my coaches for my slower times. In reality it was my fault. Not doing cross-country in the fall had surprisingly affected my track performance in the spring. I knew this in my heart but wasn't willing to take the blame. It was also hard for another reason. Mr. J was diagnosed with late-stage leukemia my senior year. I'll never forget him telling us he wouldn't be at the state meet.

It hit me hard. Track was literally the only thing I was good at. My mom worked, and my dad was in the truck, so I never had family around to cheer me on at meets. My logical brain said Mr J was the coach so he had to be there, I couldn't help but feel he was there *for* me.

The North Dakota State Track and Field Championship my senior year was held in the spring of 2003. Since I was not having a stellar season, I only remember running the in the mile relay, where each runner runs a 400-meter leg. I was the third leg. The first two runners were a bit slow, and we were behind by the time I got the baton. I had to play catch up. Since it was my only race of the meet and the last of my high school days, I ran hard.

I handed off the baton to Brittany for the anchor leg, hoping she could get us there. She was by far the best runner on the team. I got off the track, planning to cheer her on, but couldn't breathe. I thought I was going to puke. All of a sudden Brittany was next to me. The race was over, and I had no idea if we placed. Between gasps of breath I tried telling tell her I was going to throw up. Clearly, she didn't understand me since no garbage can was brought over.

After finally pulling myself together, I sauntered back to our camp area, still a bit lightheaded but fine. My coaches were reporting our splits. "One of you ran under a sixty-second leg." I looked over at Brittany; obviously it was her ... "You got yourself a personal best, Becky."

Somehow I had run the fastest.

Since Mr. J was not able to attend our state meet, we got to meet up with him at the hospital where he was getting treatments before heading back home. Someone mentioned the relay and talked about how well I ran. His dark eyes, even though you could see the fatigue behind them, still lit up. He was proud of me. I don't think I cried right then, but it was a profound moment for me. So impactful in fact that I later had his name tattooed on my forearm to always have a visual reminder that someone out there believed I am capable of more.

Graduation was a short time later. Right after that, I shipped off for my five months of Army training. On August 16, 2003, the day after my birthday, I was getting ready for the M16 rifle qualification. Mail was handed out as we were getting ready. During training mail was like gold, your only connection to the outside world. I was excited to see I had received a card, especially because it was near my birthday.

I opened the card from my mom. Instead of money or some other treasure, a newspaper clipping slid out. I saw Mr. J's face. It was his obituary. I didn't get past his name; I couldn't bring myself to read anymore. The world paused, everything went blurry. I just sat on my bunk and cried.

I still have the card with his obituary in it, still unread.

8

Becoming A Soldier

T wo major things happened in Mr. Goffe's history class that were the bookends of my junior year. In September I watched the Twin Towers fall after the terrorist attack on 9/11. I remember being confused when I walked into class that the TV was on but quickly realized something big was happening. The other bookend is that I become a soldier.

A couple of North Dakota Army National Guard recruiters came and talked to us during Mr. Goffe's class. They asked if we had a plan to pay for college. I did not. I honestly hadn't thought about it much. I had no idea what I wanted to do. I had no idea where I wanted to go. I had never pictured myself in college. My sister Pam was the only one who went to college. Ken worked right out of high school, and Amanda was a mom. *What do you want to do with your life after graduation?* wasn't a conversation we had in our family. Survival was more important than education.

The recruiters passed out half-sheet contact cards. We had to check a box if it was okay for the Army to contact us. I think that was the moment in my life where my intuition and Universe worked together and took over. I had no thoughts, good or bad; I just checked the box. At that time my mom and I had moved to a farm just a few miles southeast of Valley City. I was making myself an after-school snack in the kitchen when one of the recruiters called. I must have still been under the spell of the Universe because when he asked if I would like to join the Army National Guard, I said sure.

"I just don't want to go to training this summer."

Heaven forbid I miss out on the many fun activities between my junior and senior year.

"We can do that," he said. "Can you come in tomorrow with your mom?"

I was only seventeen, so I needed her to sign off. After a final exchange of info, I hung up. I don't remember thinking or worrying about anything, or having any reaction at all. Yes, it was a thing that most people don't do. But I felt different than most people, so it just seemed to fit.

I finished making my snack and walked into the living room. "Mom, I'm joining the National Guard."

I had no idea how she'd respond. Maybe she would say: *Oh, I'm so proud of you.* Maybe she would hug me with tears in her eyes and say: *I knew you would be the one to do something great.* No, that is not what happened. Not even a little.

"So you want to be like your brother?!"

I'm sure food dribbled out as my mouth hung open in confusion. "What are you talking about?"

She looked at me like I was the crazy one. "Your brother joined a few months ago. He's in Missouri right now for training."

I literally had no idea my brother had joined the National Guard months earlier. Granted, he's seven years older than me and lived in a different town, but still. All of a sudden, I experienced a feeling—annoyance. I wanted to be the one who was different. Instead my mother accused me of being like my brother. I didn't want to be like any of my siblings. *Dammit!*

Regardless of my annoyance, Mom and I went to the armory the next day and signed the papers. After passing all my initial exams and tests, I became a soldier on May 22, 2002. On one of my first drill weekends, Staff Sergeant Amy Weiser came around and asked me some questions for their monthly newsletter. I easily answered most except for one.

"Why did you join the Army National Guard?"

I had no idea. I didn't have a plan for college. So really it wasn't about college money. I didn't have special patriotic feelings, so it wasn't for God and country. My dad only briefly served as well as my grandpas, but it wasn't a family tradition to serve. I had no logical reason to do it. It just felt like the thing to do.

Only as I began to understand my intuition, did I finally realized I do have an answer to the question: *Why did you join the Army National Guard?*

Because my intuition told me to.

9

You're Going to War, Private

Okay, people, laser focus now. The year was 2003. The United States invaded Iraq in March. I graduated high school in June and was off to Army basic training in July. Like most soldiers, I went straight to my specific army job training—supply 92Y—from September to November.

Fun fact: I could disassemble and reassemble a 9mm pistol faster than my classmates and instructors. No big deal. You still following me? Clearly I got distracted by my ego. Okay, I'm focused again.

In October while still at training, my drill sergeant called me out of morning physical training and said I needed to talk to the National Guard Liaison.

I shouted the obligatory reply: "Yes, Drill Sergeant!" having no idea what a liaison was.

I learned a National Guard liaison is the go-to person between the guard unit back home and the training facility you're at. This liaison had received a notification.

"Your unit has been mobilized for Operation Iraqi Freedom. You'll be deploying to Iraq in December. Here are your orders."

What the fuck?! is what I said in my head; what came out of my mouth was: "Roger, Sir."

I feel I should clarify that *roger* was not his name; it's a term that means yes in military lingo. I've made the mistake before of assuming people know that. It can make for awkward conversations, let me tell you.

I walked out of the liaison's office with weirdly mixed feelings of excitement and confusion. Almost giddiness. Missing were anxiety and fear. *What the hell is wrong with me? Shouldn't I be more concerned? I was just told I'm going to war. War is bad. People die. Normal people should be scared or nervous. I'm not. What the hell is wrong with me?*

I didn't know then, but I understand now, that I wasn't scared because it was the path I was supposed to take. My intuition provided comfort and let me know it was the right thing. I was on the right path.

I reported back to my drill sergeant, who had a sly smile. "You're going to war, aren't you, Private?"

"Yes, Drill Sergeant."

Then I fell into cadence with my fellow soldiers doing side-straddle hops.

I got home from training at the beginning of November. Our original deployment date was December 3, but it got pushed back, and we left a couple of days after Christmas to Fort Carson, Colorado, to train up. Just a couple of short months later, I found myself halfway around the world in a war-torn country. I was nineteen years old, riding a multi-day convoy through the heart of Iraq; a country we invaded less than a year earlier. We had homemade welded armor plates on the sides of our trucks to protect us from gunfire and roadside explosives. I had a rifle by my side that never shot anything but a paper target. I had old, green camouflaged protective body armor over my desert sand-colored camouflaged uniform. This protected me from direct fire or shrapnel but no actual camouflaging into my environment. My clunky helmet bobbled and bounced between my required bun hairstyle and the frames of my new glasses—which were now taped after getting crushed during the sardine-packed, thirty-nine-hour flight to Iraq in a C130.

Somehow I was at ease. How could riding through a war zone in sweltering heat feel more comfortable than the rest of my life so far? The most discomfort I felt was my overwhelming need to poop during the convoy. I seriously thought I would have to poo in a MRE (meal-ready to eat) bag in the front seat of the humvee with three other people in it. We made it to a checkpoint in time, but I can't tell you how miserable that was. I literally cried because of how scared I was of having to poop in front of other people.

Somehow through all of those surface struggles and worries, I didn't have an underlying, unexplainable anxiety during my year in Iraq. I was in a country where Al Qaeda was trying to kill me so I obviously had some anxiety about that, but it wasn't the same. I never questioned what my purpose was. I had no clue what was my purpose, but I didn't feel I needed to know. Everything was what it was.

It's a strange thing to process that I felt comfort being deployed but didn't feel comfortable on a social level. It was an internal struggle that never evened out. I tried hard to be accepted with the rest of the supply soldiers. My intuition provided me comfort about being at war, but I had very little comfort being socially accepted.

Lana, Tracy, Kari, Nicole, and I were known as the Supply Girls. There was Bob too. He was a cook, but since we didn't need cooks on this deployment, they just assigned the cooks to other sections. We got Bob. Bryan was our supply sergeant and boss. God bless him for dealing with all of us females—and Bob.

We all had roles. In high school I was the funny, silly friend. I felt comfortable making people laugh and smile. I was able to be myself. In Iraq, I didn't have that. That role was already taken. Lana was the silly one. I absolutely adored her. She seemed so comfortable with herself, most of the time, anyway. I literally felt I could feel her buzzing when anxiety got the best of her. Traci was our quiet mom for a hot minute until she got sent home because she was pregnant. She had been pregnant before we even left the States. She was one of those strange anomalies where peeing on stick results in a false negative. She was sent home two days after a blood test finally confirmed what she already knew. Nicole was the responsible one. She took over the mom role after Traci left.

Kari was our middle child. She often did her own thing but was still part of the crew. Since I was the youngest and the freshest from training, I got the baby role. Sure, I'm the youngest of my family, but my family role was much different than the military baby role. My role fit my purpose, I think, but it was hard to be myself. I often tried too hard and would hear myself say something crazy. Everyone would give one another a side glance, and I would slowly creep out of the room.

As awkward and strange as I felt socially there, I began to evolve tremendously as a person. My confidence to accomplish things I'd never dream of doing grew. I learned to back up a trailer. It took two months, but I was finally able to perfectly maneuver my two-and-a-half-ton truck to drop and unhitch the water buffalo. It was a victorious moment.

I began to understand how things change when you leave your comfort zone. I discovered a whole new world. A dazzling place I never knew. (If you didn't sing that, I'm disappointed in you.) I grew to love trashy romance novels. People would often send us care packages. One of the problems of war is fighting off boredom. We ended up creating a library of donated books. Romance novels seemed to be the most common genre. I was hesitant at first but was encouraged to give one a try. I was immediately addicted. They're fun, easy reads that give you break from real life. If you haven't given one a try, please do.

It was also a time of self-reflection. My journal entries are filled with life and purpose questions. I had intuitive moments written throughout my journals. I never said: *Here is an intuitive thought I had.* But I wrote things, like: *I had a strange feeling the last time I saw him, I knew he wasn't coming home with us."*

I often tried to figure out what I wanted to do when I got home. I pondered relationships, friends, career, and life in different cities and countries. Perhaps the Universe knew I needed to grow outside of North Dakota.

On most deployments of more than a year, soldiers are given two weeks of leave. Vacation time if you will. You could fly anywhere on the Army's dime. I had some friends go to Hawaii. My brother went to Germany. I regrettably chose to go home. In the end it was probably for the best because it was eye-opening and it was then I knew North Dakota would never be my home.

August 2, 2004
 So I know it's been a very long time since I have written. That is

because I just got back from leave. It was good. I learned a lot I think. It was not what I had expected. I hardly drank or partied. I realized a lot in those fifteen days. Nothing has changed back home, which could be good, but not when I have changed.

I talked to Allison about this. It just didn't feel like I belonged anywhere there. I can't go back to how I was. That won't get me anywhere. Holly and LaMoure? Not in a million years. Too country for me. I really just need to find myself a place. That's why I guess I didn't mind coming back to Iraq. I belong here. I really feel like I have nothing back home. I know I have a mom, my family, my car,[2] and Speed Bump of course, but that is not a life. That is just part of life. That is the only part that I am certain about. Nothing else really makes sense.

I mentioned in the journal entry about Holly and LaMoure. Here's the story behind why. I visited her on my leave. She was dating this new guy I had never met before. I was dating a guy overseas, but it was for entertainment purposes only—hey, like I said, there's a lot of boredom in war. We were sitting outside her house talking when her boyfriend pulled up in his truck. She introduced me. I said hello.

His response to me was, "I hear you fucked a nigger."

Not a: *Hi, nice to meet you,* just instant racism. I immediately hated her boyfriend. I didn't even pretend to be nice. I can't remember what happened afterward, if I left or what, but I do remember saying to myself: *Fuck this place.*

---

[2] I bought my car on EBay from California. My sister, Amanda, and I flew out there during my leave and then drove it back. It was the highlight of my two-week leave.

10

Moving to the Big City

I got home from Iraq in February 2005, and by March had moved to Minneapolis-St Paul, which we affectionately refer to as the Twin Cities or just the Cities. It was big enough to be different and close enough—around a five-hour drive—to go home. Everything I owned fit into my little hatchback Acura RSX that I had bought on eBay. I found a little seven-hundred-square-foot apartment in a Minneapolis suburb called Richfield. It had a nice outdoor pool that I took advantage of maybe five times. All my notifications came in Spanish first then English.

I worked briefly for a resource magazine that sold advertising space to businesses. I had to do a lot of cold calling, which meant I got some nasty, negative responses and a lot of rejection. In my head I knew it wasn't personal—they weren't saying no to me—but I still took it to heart. Reading the paper one day, I saw a tiny, six-line advertisement for hypnotherapy. There goes that Universe jumping in and directing me. I had no logical reason to want to see a hypnotherapist or even see those few lines of advertisement out of the entire newspaper. But I did.

Off I wandered in the evening into the basement of a stranger after seeing a classified ad in the paper. Since it wasn't on the back page, I felt the likelihood of being murdered was minimal. Without realizing it I was trusting my intuition because logically the cards were stacked against me.

She happened to be very kind and generous. We talked for a bit, and she showed me some cool stuff with flower essences, picking some out for me based on our conversation. When the session began, she had me hold a different bottle with my eyes closed. Per her direction she asked me to say something if I started to feel any changes in my body. I was holding one of the bottles and felt a weird tingle in my lower back. I looked at the bottle and sure enough, it was specifically for that.

Holy cow, how neat-o!

If you've never been hypnotized, it's a really strange sensation. You are fully aware of everything around you. I felt her cat jump on my lap. I could hear what she was saying. I didn't feel like I was out of body or anything. It was very relaxing. Time is lost though. She asked how long I thought I was under and I guessed seven minutes. It was about forty. During the session, she said that the color purple would be bright and significant as long as I would like it to be. *Cool.*

As the session came to a close, I was feeling great—optimistic and light. I said thank you as I climbed the steps and happened to notice the rug on the stairs. It caught my eye, and I commented to her how much I liked it. She smiled sweetly and led me out.

Driving home from the appointment I replayed the session in my head. Then it dawned on me. The damn rug was purple! I only noticed it after she said the color purple would be significant for me.

As hard as the Universe nudged me there, I didn't take the yummy carrot that was dangled in front of me. It was an amazing experience, but my credit card bill was getting bigger, and I couldn't afford to see her again. The cold calling job wasn't working out. In the ratty old bra fashion, I had to do what I've done since I was little: I had to take care of things myself. That meant figuring out a new job and making money. That's what normal people do. I'm a normal person. I just got back from a year in Iraq. I survived there. Certainly I could survive normal life.

One day after living in the Twin Cities for about a year, I was looking out the passenger window and had a déjà vu moment as I saw the downtown skyline on an overpass on Interstate 694. It brought me back to a trip in the truck with my dad that my sister Pam and I went on when I was about ten years old. We were on our way to Wisconsin on I694, which took us through the Cities. I was sitting in the front seat, excited because I had never seen a big city before. We came over a small hill on an overpass, and I saw the Minneapolis skyline. It was a beautiful beacon of tall, shiny buildings reflecting the light of the sun.

I said to myself: *I'm going to live there someday.*

Not only did I live in the Cities, but it wasn't long before I found a job as an office manager at a bridal shop in that beautiful downtown skyline. My childhood intuitive dream came true.

My friend Cody was one of only two people I knew when I moved to the Cities. We reconnected and he started coming over more and more. Somehow he magically started living with me. He and his tortoise, Louis, moved right in. At that point I had adopted a beautiful golden mini-lop bunny named Piper, but everyone just called him Bunny. He was an ass. But he was incredibly adorable and litter trained, so I didn't care. If Louis was out and about, she would find her way into Bunny's cage, and I kid you not, those two became best friends. When I went to move Louis back into her tank, Bunny would snap, glare, and snarl, his bunny way of saying: *Leave my friend alone!* If you haven't picked up on the irony of this yet, this was a true life tortoise and the hare story.

Sadly, I must confess I accidentally murdered Bunny. Shortly after I bought my first house, I got the carpets cleaned. They said keep pets away for at least twenty-four hours. I waited only about twelve, thinking the floor was dry enough. I chose convenience over intelligence. Well, Bunny got sick. I took him to the vet. She said she could save him, but it would cost some dollar amount I couldn't afford. Bunny was too much of an asshole to cost me that much. Sorry, Bunny.

I enjoyed working in the bridal store and living in the city; however, I struggled financially. Managing finances was not a family strength. We generally never had any money to manage. I went from high school to military training to war. I didn't realize I had to pay for lunches and taxes. I didn't understand budgeting, and I let things get out of control. I did what I do and took care of it. I found some budgeting books at the thrift store and got busy digging myself out. I started volunteering to go on military orders so I could make extra money to pay off my debt. It turned out to be a great decision for multiple reasons but mostly because it opened the doors to full-time employment. The supply sergeant I worked with was getting a promotion, so I studied my ass off, applied for his job, and was selected. June 2006 was the start of a fourteen-year military career.

I was getting my life in order. I found a handsome guy who actually liked me enough to marry me, and we were planning our family. We even bought our dream home. Things were fitting into place. Everything was feeling right. The military career was the right path for me—for a while. Funny thing about paths, rarely do they go straight. There is always a curve, a fork, or an end.

11

A Shifted Path

There. You probably know me better than many of my friends do. So how did I, a stinky, lisp-talking, bunny slaying nobody, come to write a book on intuition? I have no logical reason to give you. The definition of intuition is *the ability to understand something immediately, without the need for conscious reasoning.* The best answer I can give you is that writing this book was just something I was supposed to do.

As hard as it may be for some to grasp this concept, we do not need to find a logical reason for everything. It's okay to say, *because my intuition told me to.* Our intuition tells us by giving us a feeling such as a deep inner understanding of something feeling right. Perhaps it's a strange "off" feeling that you can't put into words. That's good enough. Once we learn to trust those feelings, that's our green light to confidently make intuitive decisions.

I could feel that my military path was changing; I felt it was crumbling below my feet and didn't know what to do. I tried applying for new jobs in the military, but each of those roads was blocked in some shape or form. I did multiple logical and reasonable things to try and make it feel right again. Nothing was working. I wasn't being myself and didn't recognize who I was anymore. I knew I couldn't handle being on this path if it wasn't allowing me to be my authentic self. I had to trust my intuition.

I needed to figure out how to shift away from a military path toward something that felt better and not end up feeding my family to the saber-toothed tigers. I knew it would be difficult and against all logic, but I knew I had to be true to myself. I felt if I stayed on my current path much longer, the path would crack or it would shatter; I would be swallowed up and my true self, lost forever.

I realized what I had to do. I had a glass of wine (or two) and sat my husband down in our formal dining room with my homemade blue curtains. I looked around at our dream home. When we bought it I was thirteen-weeks pregnant with our first, and when I walked in the front door the first time, it had a big, open staircase with its white, wooden rails. I could see our kids walking down, all dressed up for their first dances and proms. The home that we brought both of our babies home to. Victor in 2012 and Lily in 2014. The four-thousand-square-feet home that hosted birthdays, holidays, and parties. The home that was absolutely perfect with everything we wanted.

I looked at him, took a long drink of my cabernet, and asked if we could sell it all. I figured if we cut our mortgage in half, I could leave my steady, salaried, guaranteed-retirement-after-twenty-years job with amazing health benefits so I could pursue something else, although I didn't know exactly what that something else was quite yet.

Needless to say, we didn't talk for about a week. But after coming to terms and figuring it out, we sold our dream home in 2016, and the Universe teamed up with my intuition and took the reins.

I'm not suggesting to sell your house. I'm not saying you should leave your job because you may be unhappy or don't like it. That's not why I left the military. There was a different, unexplainable feeling; I knew the military path wasn't the one I was supposed to be on anymore. I knew it was time to find a new path.

12

Purple-Laced Punches

I n 2014 I was pregnant with our second child. My first pregnancy went well. The only issue during the second pregnancy was out-of-control seasonal allergies. I could not step outside without my face puffing up and feeling like I was suffocating. So I did what many people do—turned to Facebook to complain. A dear friend of mine, Josie, responded to my complaint. She asked if I'd ever tried essential oils. I'd never heard of them, but her friend was hosting a class to learn about them. At that point I was willing to try anything, so I said yes I would go check them out.

As the class date drew closer, I started to talk myself out of going. I came up with every excuse: *It's a forty-minute drive. It's a direct-selling company, so I'll be tricked into buying into something. I don't know this person.* I was tired, stuffy, and just not sure I was up for meeting new people. But there was that little thing inside that managed to keep my feet moving out the door and to Anoka for an essential oil class.

It was a very positive experience. The essential oils worked! I felt relief almost instantly, and I loved the class and everyone there. I actually loved it so much that I ended up building an essential oil business. I taught classes on oils and did many craft and vendor shows for about two years. I learned so much about personal development and growth that I started to dive deep into my strengths as a leader. This path was feeling great.

Then, of course, the Universe stepped in again and thought it was time to curve the path a bit more, a bend so slight that I didn't notice right away that it was shifting. It was at one of the craft and vendor shows where the Universe nudged me on this curved path. It was up to me to listen to the nudge.

At one particularly large vendor show, our booth was next to a wonderful woman selling mala beads and offering chakra checks. I didn't know what chakras were, but she explained them as seven major energy points that help balance and control the functions in our bodies. She held a pendulum over my chakra points, and it would either spin in a circle, move in a straight line, or come to a dead stop, depending on whether my chakras were blocked or flowing. I thought that was pretty nifty. It was really eye-opening to learn about chakras and how important they are to our everyday functions. The issues she pointed out were definitely things I knew I could work on.

A month later I was at a different and much smaller vendor show. I was hosting this show at the armory I worked at. One of the vendors came up and asked me for the WiFi password. Her name was Marie, and I noticed she had some bracelets that looked like the colors of the chakras I had just learned about the month before. Since I had been working on the issues that were pointed out, I asked if she did chakra readings so I could see if they had changed or not. Marie said she could check my chakras for me, so when the event winded down, I went to her booth. It was simple, with some crystals, stones, and books for sale along with some flyers and business cards displayed on a white table cloth. She directed me to come around and sit in the chair across from her. I told her about my previous chakra experience.

"Okay, let's see how they're doing." She took a purposeful breath and closed her eyes.

"Whoa, what are you doing? Where's your pendulum?" I asked. She smiled and explained she could see them.

Uhm, okay. I'd never had a reading and didn't know anything about it, so I was excited and nervous. Going through each of my chakras, she amazed me. She was very accurate and pulled a couple of things out of nowhere that blew me away. One of the things she told me was that I was a healer.

Yeah, sure lady. What does that even mean?

She also said I had some excited people around me, which creeped me out at first. She said they had been waiting to talk to me. These were my spirit guides.

I left her table a mix of feelings. How did she know specifics? I totally understand how the Barnum theory works, which is applying personal meaning to vague statements. It's a common thing that happens with psychic readings and horoscopes. But Marie had told me things that were specific, not vague and couldn't be simply explained away. Being the logical, rational, skeptical person I am, I wanted to devise a way to test the legitimacy of what she said.

I began researching and reading about psychics, spirit guides and their legitimacy. Very serendipitously, a few weeks later a friend posted about a book she had just read and loved: *The Universe Has Your Back.* I recognized the author on the cover, Gabby Bernstein, from some of the videos I had watched. Without thought—so in other words, intuitively—I downloaded it into my Audible account and started listening during my drive time. It was a knock-your-socks-off, aha moment packed book. In one of the chapters, Gabby guides you on how to pick a sign from the Universe to use when you need guidance or feel stuck.

As I pulled into my garage, the narrator, being Gabby herself, said, "It's now time for you to pick your sign."

I saw one of my kid's kickballs in a wagon. The first thought that came into my head was purple. The ball was a specific shade of purple, and I decided that was my Universe sign and wanted to test it out. I had been contemplating seeing another psychic and thought this would be an excellent chance to test my new sign.

One issue with readings is they are a bit expensive. Money was tight, so I was really debating whether I should go see another psychic or not. I found a local metaphysical shop on its psychic Tuesday, the day the psychic was in the shop and taking appointments for readings.

Activating my sign, I said in the emptiness of my kitchen, "Universe, if I'm supposed to go see the psychic today, please send me my sign." Then I left to go run some errands.

I was just getting off a roundabout by my house when the most purply purple car was waiting at a stoplight. Not only was this car purple, it was the exact shade of my purple kickball sitting in my garage.

What the hell?

I had never seen the car before and there it was right in the neighborhood where I had lived for nearly two years. I was digging for logic and reason to see a purple car right then. I couldn't find any. It still took me until an hour before my last chance of an appointment to go see Deb at the psychic Tuesday event, but with Gabby's voice in my head, I trusted the sign and went.

I walked in, shook Deb's hand, and sat down at the small table in the center of the room. There wasn't any crazy crystal ball in front of her like I had imagined there might be, just a nice tablecloth with a few stones and crystals. She didn't have a wrap or turban on her head. She wore a black blouse that complemented her short, wavy blonde hair. It felt authentic and not a room that Miss Cleo created. The same feelings of excitement and nervousness ran through me like at my last reading. She asked what I would like to get out of the session. I was honest and explained how I randomly met with another psychic who had said some things, and I wanted to know more.

Deb then said, "Did she tell you that you're a healer?"

What. The. Fork. "How did you know?"

Deb said she felt it when we shook hands.

Okay, lucky guess; but you have my attention.

She also said I had some very excited spirit guides, along with some other interesting things. As she continued on with her reading, she stopped abruptly.

"They keep showing me the color purple; does that mean anything to you?!"

My jaw dropped. I checked to see if I was wearing anything purple. Nada. *How in the world …*

She didn't understand why I was freaking out, so I then explained the whole situation; I even showed her a picture of the vision board I had done earlier that week, which included the words *the power of purple*.

I left the reading sort of confused but comfortable, yet still not completely convinced; there had to be a reason behind it all. So I decided to do another test. I called my mom.

"Mom, on a scale of one to ten, what would you rate your psychic abilities?"

"Oh, I suppose about a three, but if I were to actually try, maybe a seven."

"Do you think it runs in the family?"

"Yeah, it does. My great grandma was considered a witch because she could heal people."

Well shit. Now, my mom has the propensity to exaggerate and falsely recall stories, so even if that witch thing wasn't true, it was still very serendipitous she said it without knowing why I was calling. I'm sure my guides high-fived, fist pumped, and shouted, *"Finally!"*

During the first meeting with the psychic Marie, when I found out I was a healer, she also said I should look into doing the *raindrop technique,* a method of using essential oils on the feet and spine to support many body systems. Since she had been spot on about the healer thing, along with many other observations, I decided to listen. The other psychic, Deb, told me I should look into *Reiki* as well, a form of hands-on energy healing. She also mentioned a local community college that had an integrative and holistic healing program. Since I'm an obliger and rule follower, I became a raindrop practitioner, a Reiki master, and started the IHH degree program.

As I started on this holistic path, I began to understand some things. Many of the classes in the IHH program didn't have standard homework assignments. Instead I had to go spend two hours in nature for one then for the next, I had to unplug my electronics for twenty-four hours. I had to get creative with projects like making a prayer flag and drawing a self-portrait. I began to understood experiencing was the most valuable thing I could do. I had to experience my intuition in order to find answers. Knowledge is limited. No book—including this one—can fully get someone to understand intuition. We need to experience things instead of just reading about them. Would I want a doctor who has just read a book on surgery to remove a kidney? Hard pass.

I continued testing my sign from the Universe, the color purple. I was doing a small vendor show in a mall. A few booths down was Ray the Rock Man. He had crystals, stones, fossils, and a lot of fun, earthy creations. I was quite fascinated by it all although I had no indication of whether stones and crystals really did anything *The Crystal Bible* claimed they did.

Ray directed me to relax and just point to one or two rocks that drew my attention. I eyed the table and picked up two different rocks that appeared shiny to me. He opened his rock bible, and I read about my chosen rocks. I was dumbfounded; they seemed to be exactly what I needed.

Then I heard a tiny voice in the back of my head shout out: *If I buy a crystal because it supposedly supports healing, would I just be one step closer to wearing a tie-dyed shirt with bedazzled butterflies?* Somehow—and thankfully—my intuitive voice was a bit louder, so I decided to ask the Universe for some help.

I took a piece of paper and wrote down: *Do I need to get one of the crystals or stones from Ray today?* I folded it up, held it in my hand, and asked the Universe to show me my sign if I did. I added an extra: *Could you be quick with the sign since we only have a couple of hours left before the show closes up.*

Supposedly we shouldn't rush the Universe, but a timely

decision needed to be made. I watched a couple of purple things go by—a coffee mug, a scarf, and a shirt—but none of these items were bright or stood out to me. About twenty minutes after my pleas for guidance to the Universe, I was glancing over at the booth behind me that was selling home-sewn products. I saw a woman in a yellow sweater with a purple Minnesota Vikings reusable bag. It looked super shiny to me.

I got a little excited thinking it was my sign, but it wasn't my exact shade of purple so I said, "Universe, is that my sign, or do I just want it to be my sign, so therefore I think it is my sign?"

Not three seconds after I asked that, the yellow sweater woman picked up a blanket from the table in front of her. It was the exact shade of purple as my sign from the Universe. I got an incredible miracle moment and didn't even have to put on a bedazzled butterfly tie-dyed shirt. I could access this amazing world just being me. I only had to ask and trust the signs that were given.

How freaking simple. Literally anyone could do what I did.

Intuition really works in our favor when we're open and willing to trust. I went to see my chiropractor of eleven years and got there a bit early. Dr. Amanda Kelsey was chatting with her last client, discussing how she wanted to rent her extra exam room to a massage therapist but wasn't being too proactive about it. Without any thought I said I would be interested in renting it to do raindrops and energy work. I hadn't thought about it before, but here was an opportunity laid out in front of me, and the Universe apparently thought I should take it. She agreed and that's how my official holistic healing business got started. I added massage to my practice shortly after I launched to help drive people in the door so I could introduce them to other holistic concepts.

I opened the business before I was technically ready but felt it was right. I'm a quick learner, and Dr. Kelsey was a wonderful mentor. Marie Forleo, an amazing life coach, motivational speaker, and web television host of an inspiring show called *Marie TV* says, "The key to success is to start before you are ready." Clearly, you have to be smart about it and have your ducks in a row, but I knew I would become better by experiencing my practice.

I learned something new with each healing or massage session I experienced. I stopped doing massage and energy work full-time to focus on writing this book. I still do energy work but no longer massage. Even though my business is no longer my focus, the experience was priceless. It was a short path but a right one.

13

The Universe Is a Shitty Kid

Perhaps the Universe is the most patient and understanding force out there. I didn't budge on its first attempt at getting my attention. I didn't even look its way. Maybe it forgave me and just waited until the next time I wasn't busy. Or maybe it's a shitty kid throwing a tantrum in the middle of a grocery store until they get the damn cookies. Except the grocery store is your life and the cookies are your purpose.

I've come to the conclusion it's a shitty kid. I've dealt with enough kids, including my own, to recognize the signs.

"Mom, Can I have a snack?"

"No."

"Can I have a snack, *please?*"

"No. You just had breakfast ten minutes ago."

(Throws evil glare)

"But I want a snack!"

"No. Snack time is when the little hand is on the ten."

(Stomps feet and waves fists wildly in air)

"I need a snack now!"

Or this one.

"Mom…Mom…Mom…Mom…Mom…Mom."
"What?"
"I love you."

If we don't acknowledge or listen, just like kids, the Universe will keep trying to get our attention until we finally look. And the funny thing is that once we look, we realize it wasn't a big deal—*I love you. Can you help me? Look at the picture I drew.* And we wonder why we just didn't listen in the first place instead of getting all annoyed and angry.

I'm telling you the Universe works the same way. We can keep ignoring the signs and the Universe will keep pestering us until we get so annoyed that we just scream. We shout, "why can't I get a break?"

But then, just like a tantrum child, the Universe says, *I love you* and give you a big hug. It's there, but we have to be looking for it.

Let's say it's time for a new car, and you find a sweet gangster ride that the common folk call a Honda Odyssey. You're pumped, excited. You'll get thumbs up and side glances as you cruise the streets. As you are looking for these thumbs up and nods of approval, you see another Odyssey go by. *Mine is more awesome.* Then another goes by. And another and another and *Holy hell, when did all these Honda Odysseys get on the road?*

Is it the year of the gangster minivan ride? The answer is no. The roadways have been filled with Odysseys since 1995. So why has it taken you over twenty years to notice them? Easy—because you weren't looking. It's likely the Universe and our own intuition have always been trying to get our attention; we just haven't looked or listened.

It works the same for negative things as well. You know that old saying: *bad things happen in threes?* Whoever said that first should have been punched in the throat. Why do two more bad things happen after the first? Because we are looking for them. We have a voice in our head that says: *Bad things happen in sets of three. You better watch out.* Yes, certainty watch out and guess what? You will find them. Try this; next time a negative event happens, hear a new motto in your head: *Great things are just around the corner.* Make it as cheesy as possible so it gets stuck in your head—like the Meow Mix jingle. *Meow, meow, meow, meow.* (You're welcome.) It will likely take a few times before we can fully shut off the bad-things-in-threes storyline, but I believe we can.

I also believe the Universe is a shitty kid because things will never fully work out for us if we aren't doing what we are supposed to be doing. The Universe constantly wants us to do things for our highest good. And if we don't ... ugh.

As I have mentioned before, the Universe always has the best of intentions and knows what our purpose is. So if we're playing on our cell phones instead of playing with our child, what does that child do? Yup.

As we go on with our lives and things just aren't working out, it's easy to assume we're not listening to the tantrum the Universe is throwing. Lets put down our damn cell phones and listen. Lets ask the Universe to go on a nice walk in nature. Nature is a good place to start. Let's give some one-on-one attention that the Universe has been begging us for.

Let's say you want to find love. So you pray for someone to come into your life or you just exclaim it to an empty room. Whatever floats your boat. Either way the Universe is always listening. And when you ask for help, it gets excited. By asking you have given permission, and it gets to work. Let's imagine this scenario …

Betty has been alone since her divorce. The dating sites aren't working, and she's doesn't get out much. Fed up, Betty exclaims before getting out of bed one morning: I JUST WANT TO FIND SOMEONE TO GROW OLD WITH. Betty gets to work and then Betty gets fired. She is beside herself; she needs money and doesn't have a job. Now she needs to find a new job as soon as possible.

Luckily for Betty, she just started to learn about intuition and how to trust it. She sees a job listing, but it is out of town and out of her normal career goals. But it feels right even though it goes against all logic and reason. She feels desperate and scared, but she wants to finally do the thing that feels right. She applies for the job and is hired. The hassle of moving and a career change has gotten Betty down and has her questioning her decision. But there is that little spark inside that makes her feel everything will be okay. On her first day of work, she is introduced to a gentleman named Derek, who happens to be single and awesome. They have a spark and BOOM, Betty finds love.

The Universe is always listening. We may not understand the path, but trust that it is working for our highest good. You may not understand why your kid is screaming and hollering in the middle of the store, and you may not know what the Universe's tantrum is about either, but if we pay attention and listen carefully, the purpose behind the tantrums may become clear.

14

Frozen in Fear

I'm on this new holistic path, ready to run, wanting all of these miracle moments to pour in, but a strange sense of fear comes out of nowhere, and I can't move. I'm terrified I'm missing miracle moments, and I'm screwing it all up. I'm excited and feel ready even though I'm scared, so why can't I run full force into accessing my full intuition?

There are so many things that stop us from reaching our optimal self and listening to our intuition. The list will vary for everyone. For me the obvious conscious fear was my need for acceptance. I was terrified of what people would think of me. If they knew the real me—the healer me—what would happen? I was terrified of losing loved ones and friends. I had spent my whole life fitting in with the crowd. I generally had found the balance of being myself and assimilating to social situations as needed. I know I can't drop F-bombs at my Toastmasters club meetings. I can't jam out to Taylor Swift at a biker bar. I felt if I told people, if people knew about this side of me, I'd lose all of that. I'd lose everything.

I'm still working on this fear. I'm doing alright, I suppose, since your in the midst of a book based on everything I've been scared to tell people. So really, I'm either facing my fear head on to overcome it, or the Universe has a horribly painful lesson for me to learn. Probably a little bit of both.

Since I'm stilling figuring it out, I decided to talk to someone that knows a lot more about fear than me.

I spoke to Zack Anderson, a tarot card reader on the subject of fear and intuition. He's studied and practiced tarot reading for more than fifteen years. From his experience the number one thing that people fear most about intuition is that people will hear what they don't want to hear. They are scared that if they choose to really listen to what their soul wants and what their spirit is telling them, then they could start to second-guess their own judgments of life and situations. They could realize they should leave their unsatisfying marriage or they might realize how long its been since they were satisfied with the job they settled for. They avoid their own reality. Zack summed it up by saying, "People are avoiding existential angst when they deny their intuition."

I was avoiding being fed to the saber-toothed tigers. But another fear I was avoiding was one that I wasn't even aware of. One that society had subconsciously placed in my head and likely yours. I was terrified I would become batshit crazy.

One of my first thoughts after the opportune meeting with the psychic was: *Who can I tell about this that would believe me? Who will not judge me and call me crazy?* The list was short. I'll talk like a pirate all day to a stranger and not worry about judgment, but if I told people a psychic told me I was a healer—nope.

Since there was such a big disconnect between my need for acceptance and my need to access my intuition, I had to understand why. I knew there must be some subconscious fears that were stopping me and preventing my awesomeness from reaching its max. I began researching fear and discovered a TED Talk by Tim Ferriss. In it he talks about *fear-setting*. Instead of setting goals, you set out your fears so you can plan for them.

The gist with fear-setting is to write down your fear then break it down into the worst that could happen. Then you ask what can you do now to minimalize the fear, and if it does happen, what do you do?

Every time I travel via airplane, I plan a worst-case scenario of the plane crashing. I look around to see the people I could try and save. I'm the person who turns around to see if the closest exit row is behind me. Full disclosure: when it comes to the fight-flight-freeze response, my body has the flight response, and I'd probably pass the fuck out before I could save anyone on the doomed flight. Regardless, I have a plan, so I don't have to worry about it. I'll either save people, or I'll pass out and die without knowing. I'm cool with either.

Since I was already doing fear-setting every time I got on a plane, I knew the steps; I just needed to do it with my fears about my intuition.

Fear one: I'm going to lose all my friends and social circles. (Be fed to the tigers.)

Reality: There are seven billion people on Earth. There are plenty of other people I can befriend who will maybe understand me more or be more accepting. Also, who am I to judge them first? Aren't I unfair to assume they won't be my friend anymore because I'm using my intuition now? Gee, maybe I'm the asshole here. Also, friends come and go. I have friends still from high school that I love. I have friends I love dearly that I just met a year ago. It's okay that the people we hang out with change as well.

I know some people have trepidation about change, but I believe everyone should change. As we mature, we naturally start to enjoy different things than we did when we were younger. Closing down the dance clubs is something I do not enjoy anymore. My knee would kill for days and I'd hate the world until I would catch up on sleep—if I ever would.

Fear two: Fear of the unexplainable and sounding batshit crazy.

Reality: Society inadvertently makes us scared of the unexplainable. We see ghosts and haunting stories on television and in the movies. Show likes *Sabrina* and *Ghost Hunters* become the stereotype. All of the unexplainable things seemed to be the workings of something evil and demonic. (Besides Casper, obviously.) Anything that can't be logically explained is assumed a hoax, made up in your head, or the work of the devil. Intuition cannot be explained by logic and reason. Therefore, if I use my intuition, I am doing something bad. I'll see ghosts, become possessed by the devil, or people will think I'm lying or lost my damn mind.

There are a lot of bad people walking around on Earth right now. People are getting robbed, raped, and neglected on a daily basis. Bad stuff happens literally every day, thousands of times over. But many more beautiful and wonderful things happen. Often we get stuck on the bad things. The news focuses on the negative because they know how humans operate. As much as we say we want to see positive and happy stories, the television networks know statistically we are more apt to watch negative, trauma-filled shows and newscasts than positive ones. Ninety-five million people watched the OJ Simpson trial. It's still one of the most widely publicized events in American history.

It's not our fault that we are scared of unexplainable things. But we need to stop it—right now.

Of course something bad could happen. That's just life. Get over it. We could get hit by a bus tomorrow. We don't have time to live in such a state of fear of what *might be* when there are just too many more beautiful, wonderful things that *are*. I refuse to let any potentially bad, unexplainable things stop me from being my awesome intuitive self. I don't let my fear of being mangled to death in a car accident stop me from leaving my house. I don't let my fear of the plane going down stop me from exploring and experiencing the world. I take proper precautions. I learned how to drive. I learned to acknowledge my fear and handle it with fear-setting. I read the brochure on how to make my seat a floatation device. If we learn to manage our fears in the real world, we can learn to manage them in an intuitive world as well. I am less afraid of the unexplainable.

For me, working with my intuition goes hand-in-hand with working with energy-based healing. I believe part of my bigger purpose is working in the healing and holistic world. That is the path I have been led to. Working in the energy world is mine. You have your own path. Accessing your intuition does not mean you have to be working with energies or opening spiritual doors. You can just unlock your own purpose, which could be working as a fortune cookie writer, a nurse, or a mom. Whatever it is, it's your purpose, and it will feel right for you.

So keep that in mind for this next part. This story addresses my fear of the unexplainable head on.

One of my first experiences with an energy that didn't have the highest good intention toward me wasn't at all like I planned or expected. Because of societal stereotypes, I assumed any bad energies would possess me, make me float above my bed, and speak in some creepy, deep demonic voice. That couldn't have been further from what happened. Actually, I didn't even know it happened. I felt something, but being new to the healing world, I had no idea what.

I started volunteering at a local hospital in the Integrative Health Services unit. The staff referred us to patients for energy-based healing, hand and foot massages, essential oils, guided imagery, and such. During my orientation I shadowed other clinicians and practitioners to learn how to help in a hospital setting. We often received referrals for patients in the chemical dependency unit, who were struggling with various addictions.

We had a referral to see a woman who was very distraught that day. She wanted help calming down and handling her mental health struggles. The clinician started her energy healing session, and since I was still observing, I sat in a chair near the foot of the bed. I opened my hands in my lap to offer loving healing energy.

Almost immediately it felt like I got punched in the face. My forehead where my third eye is located started pounding. I thought I was experiencing the patient's stress, but it was a distinctly different type of headache and pain. I didn't know what to do, but it felt so tight and tangible I thought that pulling at it would help. I started to pull at the tightness like it was taffy. I felt sort of silly, but it was the only thing I could think to do. I also focused on sending calming thoughts to the patient, hoping it would help her feel calm and in turn, help me. The session ended, but my headache was still there. I talked to the clinician about what happened, but she didn't know much about what I had experienced. I was perplexed. I went home to meditate on it. Since it was lingering at my third-eye chakra, I got the idea that maybe it was my third-eye trying to open.

When that occurred I was midway into level two of my energy-based healing touch class. After that strange experience at the hospital, I was eager to talk to my instructor and classmates about it and see what they thought. This class session's focus was on a technique called mind clearing and headache clearing. Perfect; I could get feedback and get rid of the lingering throbbing headache I'd had since my shift at the hospital.

After we learned about the technique, it was our time to practice. My friend Lindsay went first and practiced the mind-clearing technique on me. When her hands were on my forehead, Lindsay said she felt as if her hands were in a wind tunnel and getting strongly pushed away. It was the opposite for me; I felt like she was pulling my head forcefully backward even though her fingers barely touched me. When she swept her fingers away to the side, I felt a really strange shift and lightness and my headache seemed to lift for a bit.

I was eager to learn the next technique for headaches, hoping that would be the final push and take care of it.

My next practice partner was Deborah. I had high hopes since I had felt the energy shifts during the mind clearing with Lindsay. Unfortunately, it didn't help as I was expecting it to. It actually made my head hurt more. I asked the instructor multiple times if we could actually hurt someone doing energy work. She assured me that if we were sending the highest good, then no.

Then what the hell are you sending me, Deborah?

So I still had the strange headache. Luckily, my friend Heidi and I had one of our monthly energy-work practice sessions on the schedule. She does some amazing things in the health and fitness side of energy work. She can tune into a person's energy and help pinpoint health issues and give suggestions on how to manage them. Heidi was one of the friends early on in my journey who I could be open and honest with and not worry about judgments.

Heidi got to work, doing her thing as I laid on the massage table in the healing room I had put together for my business. I told her about my experience with the patient at the hospital and the resulting headache.

"Aha!" she exclaimed as loudly as she possibly could in her soft, sweet voice. She then explained what this headache was about.

There were some negative entities around the woman in the hospital that kept her down. When I walked into the room sending positive light, those bad guys saw the light emanating from me. I imagine the following conversation took place. And because I am an eternal child, I envision the 1950s gangsters from *Looney Toons,* Rocky and Mugsy.

> *Mugsy, you seeing dat light over der?*
> *Yeah, Boss. Yeah, I do.*
> *Den get over dere and take care of it, will ya.*
> *Da, okay, Boss.*

And that, my friends, is how my first negative energy got attached to me. Heidi helped me clear it, and all was fine. I wasn't freaked out or scared; I just thought: Okay; now I know what it's like. And I better protect myself a bit better.

Fear setting and being prepared helped me tremendously to manage the situation. With so many more beautiful and amazing things I had experienced at that point, I didn't even flinch at this one bad experience.

The author, Elizabeth Gilbert in her book *Big Magic* asks this question: "What's your flavor of shit sandwich?" She continues on and explains what she means:

> What [Mark] Manson means is that every single pursuit—no matter how wonderful and exciting and glamorous it may initially seem—comes with its own brand of shit sandwich, its own lousy side effects. As Manson writes with profound wisdom: "Everything sucks, some of the time." You just have to decide what sort of suckage you're willing to deal with. So the question is not so much: What are you passionate about? *The question is* What are you passionate enough about that you can endure the most disagreeable aspects of the work?
>
> Manson explains it this way: "If you want to be a professional artist, but you aren't willing to see your work rejected hundreds, if not thousands, of times, then you're done before you start. If you want to be a hotshot court lawyer but can't stand the eighty-hour workweeks, then I've got bad news for you. Because if you love and want something enough—whatever it is—then you don't really mind eating the shit sandwich that comes with it."

For me, I'll eat a double-stuffed shit sandwich. I know when I tune into my intuition and healing ability, it's fucking worth it.

15

Batshit Crazy

As defined by Urban Dictionary:

A person who is batshit crazy is certifiably nuts. The phrase has origins in the old fashioned term bats in the belfry. Old churches had a structure at the top called a belfry, which housed the bells. Bats are extremely sensitive to sound and would never inhabit a belfry of an active church where the bell was rung frequently. Occasionally, when a church was abandoned and many years passed without the bell being rung, bats would eventually come and inhabit the belfry. So, when somebody said that an individual had bats in the belfry it meant that there was nothing going on upstairs as in that person's brain). To be batshit crazy is to take this even a step further. A person who is batshit crazy is so nuts that not only is their belfry full of bats, but so many bats have been there for so long that the belfry is coated in batshit. Hence, the craziest of crazy people are batshit crazy.

There is your fun fact for the day. You're welcome.
I still had to come to terms with people—including myself—thinking I had *too many bats in my belfry* for using my intuition to help direct me on my path.

One of my good friends is a psychologist. One morning we were having breakfast and chatting about my classes. She told me a story about a client she had seen many years earlier who had all sorts of issues. She said he told her that he saw the color purple around her. That he could see colors around people all the time.

I said, "He isn't crazy; he's seeing people's auras. It's the energy that is emitted around living things."

She had no idea, so she shrugged it off and mentioned he had a bunch of other mental health issues as well.

That little conversation sparked a question I was curious about: why do so many people with natural intuitive gifts have mental health issues? The simple answer is this: We as a society, have told them they are batshit crazy. We have forced them to think there really is something wrong with them.

We have associated crazy with intuitive work for too long. They are not synonymous. If a kid sees colors around people, we tell them they are imagining it or lying because we don't see it. They are led to believe they must hide that part of themselves as a way to prevent being scolded or disciplined. Whenever someone is forced to hide part of who they are, it will manifest in other ways—usually not healthy ones.

How do you respond when someone says they have seen a ghost or been visited by a loved one in a dream? Most of us would be skeptical. *Yeah, sure...* We'll ask them how much they drank, smoked, or if they are sleep-deprived. We'll try to find any logical, reasonable response to explain it away.

When people are left to fight their own battles, they might turn to substances to ease the pain or to handle the stresses of being told they're crazy for seeing ghosts. Or even just the thought of seeing colors around people scares them enough to drink the images away.

If you feel that is you; if you know someone that has turned to substances to manage their stressors; I highly recommend getting in touch with a trusted mental health provider. If that isn't a step you or they are willing to take yet, I would recommend a book by Michael Bodine titled, *Growing Up Psychic*. He is very open and candid about his substance abuse as he learned to accept his unusual gifts.

If nobody has ever told you it's okay to be yourself; that it's okay to be your intuitive self, I'm here to give you a great big hug. And I don't even like hugs. But I'll give you one because you deserve it. You have natural gifts that should have led you to a wonderful life purpose, but you never were given a chance. You are not crazy. You are fucking awesome.

The other day my husband and I watched a documentary on Netflix called *The Most Unknown*. The film connects and links nine different scientists in a chain-link fashion to see what happens. The first link was a microbiologist and a physicist. The physicist took the microbiologist to one of his elaborate testing labs, which was buried thousands of feet under a mountain in the Rockies. It looked exactly what you'd think a multi-million-dollar science lab in a mountain would look like—shiny metal boxes and gizmos; white walls lined with a variety of piping systems. The usual.

Why is a physics lab buried deep in a mountain? Cosmic silence. This physicist was studying dark matter. According to Nasa Science: "It turns out that roughly 68 percent of the Universe is dark energy. Dark matter makes up about 27 percent. The rest—everything on Earth, everything ever observed with all of our instruments, all normal matter—*adds up to less than 5 percent of the Universe.*"

In order to study this dark matter, you can't let anything interfere or potentially mess up the experiments. You need cosmic silence. No energy interference from space. Why am I telling you this? Because maybe you didn't know about that. (So really two fun facts for you today.) Maybe you had no understanding of dark matter or that some really intelligent PhD scientists are studying it deep in a mountain. I didn't either, but now I do.

We may not understand how any intuitive thoughts work or how energy fields work. We may not understand how the Universe aligns things in our lives. However, it is very likely some incredibly intelligent scientist is working to find those answers. They are even smart enough to understand the need to go inside a mountain to escape energy fields from space.

Just because we don't know, don't assume it's wrong.

One of the most surprising things in the documentary was how little each of these scientists knew about the other fields of study. They didn't know why we study the tiny microbes on the bottom of the oceans. They didn't understand how important those are to climate change and our fragile atmosphere. As a scientist they listened, asked questions, and were open to possibilities they didn't even know existed the minute before. Lets be open to discover things we didn't know could possibly exist. We don't know what we don't know.

16

Subconscious Fear

E ven after realizing my conscious fears of being rejected by my tribe, dealing with the unexplainable, and going batshit crazy, I still seemed stunted in making the most of my intuition. I had all the will and desire to eat that double-stuffed shit sandwich, but I was still stuck. Luckily for me, I was looking for an answer.

In the winter of 2018, I went to a health and holistic expo with Heidi, my fellow intuitive healer friend. As we wandered and scoped out the vendors and exhibitions, we came across a woman who was a shaman. Her booth didn't have any fancy mystical décor or presence, so I instantly liked her. Through my classes in the IHH program, we briefly learned about shamanism, which is way over my head. I can't wrap my brain around how they do shamanic journeys.

I was failing miserably at explaining it to Heidi, so we went and chatted with the shaman. Her name was Laurie Wondra. We had a wonderful conversation about what shamanism is and what Laurie does. She had to leave because she was about to speak in one of the breakout sessions. We decided to attend the session and see what she had to say. Laurie was wonderful, informative, and down to earth. She had worked in the professional world before finally doing work in the holistic world.

After watching her I decided to sign up for a quick, fifteen-minute session. It was exactly what I needed. She knew I was about to start a bachelor's program and was accurate on many other things. She also said a sense of fear of the holistic world was stopping me.

Ugh. "I don't know what I'm afraid of."

I had been working on fear but hadn't been able to pin out anything. I was frustrated and wanted to be done with fear blocking my intuition.

"I don't think it is your fear; I think it's a fear of someone else's that has been placed in you."

Oh, yeah … "My mother is afraid of everything."

My mother's fear of her own abilities had been placed on me. It's in my subconscious and messing with the personal development of my intuitive side. That annoying revelation led me to another thought: *What if I become my mother?* I love my mother, but just like I love my siblings but don't want to be them, I didn't want to become my mother in the sense of living in constant state of fear.

I think everyone deep down has mother issues. Moms are generally the most predominate nurturing figure in one's life. I had an aha moment when a friend told me a memory she had about her childhood. She was a young girl, maybe six or seven, and drew a floppy-eared puppy. She was very proud and excitedly ran to show her mom, who was on a step stool cleaning and dusting a top shelf in the living room. My friend called for her mother to look at the picture, which was clearly not the most convenient thing at that moment.

A bit annoyed, her mother took a one-second glance at the

puppy drawing her daughter proudly held up and said, "That doesn't look like a puppy," then turned away and continued to clean.

The little girl was devastated.

Fast forward forty years, and my friend realized that incident is why she associates cleanliness with bad parenting. Her house has never been fifthly, but it's usually cluttered and disorganized because she subconsciously feels tidying up means she is ignoring her kids.

If you're a mother worried about messing up your kid's life, don't worry; you have. It's just one of the shit sandwiches that comes with parenting. Being a mother is filled with countless wonderful and beautiful things. The love for our kids is unmeasurable. However, we can't be awesome 100 percent of the time. We may never fully understand how impactful our seemingly meaningless words might actually be.

This gives me comfort because I don't have to worry about screwing my kids up. No matter what, they will have some sort of mother issues. It's inevitable. My kids are clothed, fed, and taught kindness. I'm a good mother. Doesn't matter; my kids will have mother issues. And that's okay. If the biggest issue I have taken into adulthood from my mother is a sense of subconscious fear, I'm totally okay with that. I'll take it.

So I ask all mothers out there to let go of any guilt about screwing up your kids. Take comfort that in some unassuming way we all have; we are in this together. And despite how bad we think we messed up, our kids are likely doing just fine.

My mother messed me up by establishing a subconscious fear of being afraid of intuition and healing energies. For years I assumed she repressed her intuition because she was terrified of what other people thought. From the outside perspective, that was the logical assumption. Then I called and asked her about it.

"Mom, what is your fear around your intuitive side? What stops you from accessing your abilities fully?"

Her answer surprised me. "I'm scared I won't get into heaven." *What?* Mind blown.

We have never been a religious family. We got kicked out of the Catholic church when my parents divorced. My mom literally stood up in church, said, "Fuck you; we don't need a church to pray," and walked us four kids out.

Her parents weren't very religious either. I was flabbergasted that my non-religious mother said she doesn't access her true potential because she fears not getting into heaven. She said the Bible says seers are sinners and do the work of the Devil. After that conversation I started researching what the actual Christian belief is. I wasn't familiar enough with the Christian belief on the subject so I asked my friend Tiffany who is in ministry school and is a devout Christian.

She explained, "Basically it's considered witchcraft, and the Bible says to stay away from it. It has a lot to do with the spiritual realm. Seers, shamans, spirit guides, etc., are all similar, pulling their powers from the darkness." She added, "God can present himself in dreams and visions or speaking to your self-conscious. He makes himself and his plans known through events."

Now specifically for my mother, she has seen unexplainable things. She's been sitting at a table in a bar, getting annoyed by the loud people at the table next to them. When she remarked about it, her friends pointed out that nobody was sitting at that table. Now that I understood where my mother's fear was coming from, things started to make a bit more sense. My mom had seen unexplainable things that she believed would send her to hell. She blocked this part of true self because of this fear. This sadly, also blocked her intuition. We can't block or hide part of ourself and expect to be our true self. I started to see that managing all of my fears were the key to unlocking my intuition. Unlocking my intuition is the key of accepting my true self.

My friend Sam could see colors (auras) around people as a child. She said, "As a child I felt being able to see these colors around people helped protect me. My siblings and I were abused as children by my father. He was a terrible man—still is. I would always see black around him. If a person was good, I would see bright colors around them—yellows and whites."

Not many people know about her childhood trauma and her intuitive gifts because she didn't know how to explain what she saw. She didn't understand it herself. After she was able to leave the abusive situation, she felt the need to suppress her ability because the of the trauma that she associated with it. She had struggled with her self-identify because she was blocking a major part of who she is.

Sam's intuition and abilities is part of who she is. I'm not suggesting accessing your intuition is going to open doors to see spirits, ghosts, or auras. It most likely won't. What I am saying is if you have had experiences like that and shut them down, you have blocked your intuition. As you begin working on trusting your intuition, I don't want you to be afraid. I don't want a fear of the unknown, an unexplainable event, or a previous experience stop you from exploring your intuitive self.

I have been practicing and using my intuition intentionally now for a few years. Out of all the people and places I have come across, I have experienced mostly loving, caring, and compassionate energy. I would assume 99 percent of intuitive people are coming from a place of love.

Accessing your intuition can feel like a religious experience. I've gone to church enough to know how powerful that experience can be. You'll see people with arms stretched high in the sky. People say they can feel the loving embrace of God. Yes! Yes, you can. And you can feel that anywhere, all the time. That is the loving experience you can feel when you access your intuition. Accessing your intuition is an empowering act.

In the book by Michael Bodine, *Growing Up Psychic,* he tells the story of an experience with someone he referred to as a *Bible thumper.* He had answered the door to a gentleman who spoke about burning in hell, the devil, and the many disguises of Satan. He invited the gentleman in at the encouragement of his mentor, Birdie. She was very kind and let the man pitch his story. He spoke about how everyone in the house was going to burn in hell unless they repented right then and prayed for salvation. Birdie then asked the Bible thumper about some other scripture in Corinthians and other places where it mentions in the Bible about the gifts of the spirit. Birdie then looked at this gentleman and said, "Son, if you're going to sell Coke, don't talk about how powerful and strong Pepsi is. Talk about how wonderful and beautiful Coke is. You'll get more business."

If you are blocking part of who you are; if you aren't accessing your intuition fully because of fear, I am telling you that fear is blocking you from a beautiful, loving, and whole feeling. My intuition brings me closer to a loving connection with a higher source.

Our fear was likely instilled by someone trying to control us for either profit or to boost their ego. The next time you are made to feel afraid, think of who put you in that state and what they gain from your fear. What do you lose from being afraid?

We just can't rely on logic and reason. We can't even trust photographs anymore. The world is full of conflicting information. Every business and politician is trying to get into our headspace to control us by some type of fear. Whether it's fear of a terrorist attack, fear of illegal immigrants, fear of vaccines, or fear of the devil, someone is messing with our head. Take back control. Learning to use our intuition to better understand the world is the best way to take back that control.

The word intuitive often infers psychic work. This automatically causes a disconnect for some people because people don't want to be psychics. They just want to feel like they are making a good decision. Do not associate the word intuitive with being psychic. That is not what intuition is about. Intuition is that inner voice that guides us through our lives. Accessing our intuition is learning to trust that voice.

Decide to no longer live in a state of fear; it's just too fucking beautiful on the other side.

17

Intuition vs. Fear

The big question is how do we know if it's our intuition, fear, or a just a random thought? Learning to recognize your actual intuitive voice takes practice. Actually it will be easier for me to explain when it's *not* your intuition.

I shared my fear of becoming batshit crazy and that I'm a worst-case scenario planner. But I didn't tell you how far I let that go. For example, I was sitting at a red light the other day and watching a few cars with the green light turning onto the street I was on. I envisioned one of them losing control and smashing into my car at a high rate of speed. Airbags would inflate, I would be crushed up onto the curb, likely hitting the light pole that would impale the passenger side. Then there would be police, sirens, and lights and so forth. I go creepy dark and gory with this.

This is not healthy.

I do this extreme car wreck death scenario visualization more than should be considered a sane amount. I know it's a horrible thing to imagine and just as bad for my mindset. I believe what we visualize, good or bad, is likely to happen. I have to continuously work to fight against my death imaginings as soon as I realize they're happening. To get out of that headspace, I ask the kids questions, I try to visualize what's happening on the DVD that's constantly playing in the back, I creep on the drivers next to me—any shiny object to get out of that thought pattern.

How do I know it's not an intuitive thought or image? Because I am consciously aware of it. It's something I'm thinking about and planning. This is no *Final Destination* shit. Our intuition does not work on our conscious level. If our intuition wants us to avoid a car wreck, it sends us subconscious thoughts in the form of urges, feelings, or senses to do something that doesn't logically make sense. You're driving, and for some unknown reason, you have a strong urge to turn right instead of your usual left. You can't find your keys and have to spend an extra three minutes looking for them, and you find them exactly where they usually are. You get a sense to leave your house earlier than usual.

I usually go to our local YMCA to either workout or get work done. I was on my way to pick up my son after school then planned on heading up to the Y. We had just gotten a little bit of snow, but nothing crazy. Then this thought came to mind: *Don't go today*.

Now, I'm behind in my work so a couple of hours of uninterrupted time is what I need. I went through all the logical and rationalizations in my head, and I still felt: *Don't go today*. So I just went home. Even though I knew I would have to work that evening, I still felt good about my decision. The ease I felt was telling me my intuitive decision was right.

That evening I told my husband I didn't get to the YMCA and was behind, so I had to get some work done after dinner. He asked why I didn't go. I simply said, "Because it didn't feel right."

He scolded me for not sticking to a routine and getting everything done. But guess what? I trust my intuition over him any day. He puts more faith in Google Maps than his intuition.

Our kids get to have weekends on occasion at Grandma's. One Sunday we had planned to pick up the kids from her house at four o'clock. It was about 1:00 p.m. when I said to my husband, "We should go pick up the kids now." I didn't have a reason to pick the kids up early but just felt we should.

He said, "No, they're fine. Let's watch a movie before we go."

I shook off the feeling of having to leave right away and sat down to watch the movie. About an hour later Grandma called in a panic. One of the kids got hurt, and we needed to get over to her house as soon as possible.

As we got in the car and headed over, I muttered under my breath, "And that's the last time I listen to you instead of my intuition."

Ninety percent of the time, we won't know if our intuition was right. We'll likely never know the purpose of taking that right turn instead of left. That's something we need to be okay with. That need to know, that need to be right is all about ego. Our ego is an asshole and can block our intuitive thoughts, which can mess up our universal life game plan.

Learning to blindly trust something intangible without knowing if your decision was the correct one seems like asking a lot, right? It's probably a bit overwhelming.

Why don't we get some help?

18

Help for Intuitive Noobs

I love the unknown. I think uncertainty is exciting. It becomes a fun adventure or puzzle. Ever done one of those escape rooms where you have to solve a series of puzzles to get out? I know we'll make it out, but it's fun having no clue what you are walking into and figuring out all of the unknown puzzles. If you want to practice uncertainty, do a puzzle room.

Marie Forleo, one of my favorite influencers, has a quote that is constantly on replay in my head: *Everything is figureoutable.* There is no fear of the unknown because I know there is always a way to figure out whatever is there. If I can figure out a pile of ratty old bras, I can figure out anything.

Now if uncertainty is scary for you, I get it. It is. However, uncertainty is actually what frees us so our lives can go in several different directions. So many people recoil from this though. Most people want security over freedom.

There is a scene in Disney's *Finding Nemo* where Dory and Marlin are stuck in a whale's mouth. The water starts draining, and they both are holding onto the tongue, trying not to fall to the back of throat. Marlin is freaking out.

Marlin: *No. No more whale. You can't speak whale.*
Dory: *Yes I can.*
Marlin: *No you can't. You think you can do these things, but you can't, Nemo!*

Marlin realizes he has called Dory by Nemo's name and that he has been treating Dory like his son. The whale then says something and Dory lets go of the tongue. Marlin catches her before she falls.

Dory: *He said, it's time to let go. Everything is going to be alright.*
Marlin: *How do you know? How do you know something bad isn't going to happen?*
Dory: *I don't.*
Marlin finally lets go.

They get blown out of the whale's blowhole. It's all crazy and fast at first, but then they land back in the water—exactly where they needed to be. (P Sherman 42 Wallaby Way, Sydney.)

I get it. It will be absolutely terrifying to let go and listen to your intuition, especially when you have no idea what will happen. Very likely it will be nonsensical and fast at first—like you are being blown out of a whale's blowhole—but you will land exactly where you are supposed to be.

If Marlin's letting go wasn't inspiring enough, I recommend trying your own fear-setting activity. Pick out one of your fears that is blocking your intuition. Write down the worst case scenario. Next, write out what steps could be taken now to mitigate the risk. The last part is to think about what you would need to do if that worst case scenario happens. For example:

Worst case scenario: The plane crashes.

Mitigate the risk: Read the safety procedures and pay attention to flight attendants well rehearsed safety briefing. Plan to be a hero by helping people to exit rows.

If it does happen: I pass out and die. My husband gets paid my life insurance, takes the kids on an amazing vacation to help with grief, while vacationing he falls in love with a bartender and continues to live a happy life drinking fruity drinks on the beach while my kids use my loss as fuel and drive to be successful at whatever they decide to do.

Listen, I'm not going to pretend I know how to manage fears fully. I still sometimes do a quick skidaddle climbing up the stairs of a creepy basement. Managing fear is a continuous process, and I work on it all the time. If fear setting didn't help, Google *managing your fear*. You'll find a thousand books, articles, and essays on the subject. I highly recommend the book I quoted earlier about eating shit sandwiches, *Big Magic* by Elizabeth Gilbert, who also wrote *Eat. Pray. Love.* And again, you can always get assistance from mental health professionals.

When I looked back at how many big deal moments in my life were made using my intuition, it was really eye-opening. I didn't realize I was using my intuition for many of those decisions: my military career, meeting my husband, having kids, going holistic, my direct selling business. It's very possible you've done the same. Nowadays there are assessment tests for everything. We can take a test to see if we would survive a zombie apocalypse or a test to see if we are smarter than a fifth grader. The internet is full of possibilities. Right now, I offer you an assessment to see if your intuition has been guiding you and you didn't even know it. I feel this assessment may be a little more accurate than the Buzzfeed quiz titled *How Powerful Is Your Intuition?*

So without judgment or censorship, find a journal or a piece of paper and write down three to five important things in your life. Think about some of the big deal things in your life: marriage, kids, career, friendships, travel, etc.

Next, think about the pivotal steps that got you there. Was there a big move that was made? Did you get fired and have to find a new job? Was a phone call or a text message a key factor? Start with the big deal in mind and work backwards to find those three to five key steps that led to this big deal thing in your life. Do this for each moment you wrote down.

The final step is categorizing whether that important step was based off a decision you made or was it made for you? Write down if it happened because of a decision you made or someone else? For each decision that you made, write *mine*. If it was out of your control, write *someone else*.

Here is my example.

Big Deal Thing: 2002-2016 Military Career
    2006- Supply Sergeant job opened up. *someone else*
    2005 - Volunteered for ADOS orders. *mine*
    2005 - Moved to Minnesota, *mine*
    2002 - Joined the National Guard, *mine*

For each pivotal step, think back on how each of those decisive moments felt. What were you thinking when that decision was made? How did you feel? Were you fully aware you were making such a big decision?

If you do this for all of your big things in your life, you should have a good understanding of whether you have been listening to your intuition and didn't realize it. The more *mines* you have, the more you have listened. If most of those steps were made by someone else, then it's likely you've left your intuition behind and let someone else lead your life to where *they* wanted you to go.

No matter what your results are, you can start listening now. Zack Anderson, the tarot card reader, compared it to learning music. Just like anything, some people learn faster than others. Some people are just more naturally inclined with certain skills. Learning to trust your intuition is like playing an instrument. With a little practice anyone can pick up a guitar and learn to play the basic chords. Very few people are going to become like Jimi Hendrix. But people willing to practice enough are going to get to that intermediate proficiency range. You don't need to be a Jimi Hendrix of intuition. You can benefit greatly by learning the basic chords.

Basic Chords of Intuition

Step one: Decide

You have to decide to listen. Proclaim it in your journal, out loud, scream it to your cat. Do whatever, but make the decision to start to listen to your intuition. Write it right here, right now.

I_____ decide to trust my intuition fully!

Congratulations! I'm so glad you have decided to do it. That was the easy part.

Step two: Reality Check

Now, you have some work to do. I didn't spend a good portion of this book telling you about my childhood and family relationships for entertainment purposes only. Understanding the dynamics of our relationships is a critical component of intuition. You need to understand how you became you. If you can't accept the reality of your life, you can't accept those intuitive thoughts.

My dad doesn't hug me. So what? I could sit and compare him to other lovey-dovey, hugging dads and get pissed he doesn't treat me like that, but what good does it do? Nothing. Theodore Roosevelt called comparison *the thief of joy*.

I've accepted the reality that my dad shows his love through potatoes. And you know what? I fucking love it. I think my dad and I have a great relationship. Could it be better? Sure, but it's what I make of it. I call him, I go visit him, I give him hugs. I'm 100 percent responsible for the relationship that I want to have.

Recently, my husband and I had an argument. Shortly after I started scrolling through Facebook and came across this guy sitting in his car, giving some relationship advice. The Universe dropped this well-timed video for me to see. I picked up what the Universe was laying down and hit play.

The video was made by a gentleman name Eric Post.[3] He had gotten into a fight with his wife and found himself saying: *I wish my wife was more spontaneous. I wish my wife was more fun. I wish my wife was more (fill in the blank).* So Eric wrote a list of all the things he wanted his wife to be on the left side of a piece of paper. On the right side, next to each wish, he wrote down how he could help her become that. Then he did all those supportive things for two years and didn't tell her he was doing it. Guess what? She magically became all the things he wanted.

I decided to do this with my husband. I made a list of all the things I wished he would be. I then wrote how I could support him to become these things. The only difference was I sat down with my husband, and we went through the list together. He then did a list for me. We both worked on our wish lists in support of each other, and guess what? It worked and greatly improved our marriage.

Here is the key to understanding this. It's not that the other person changed. It's that we shifted the responsibility of our relationship onto ourselves. We became responsible for the relationship we wanted. If I can accept potatoes instead of hugs, I can have amazing relationships with anyone.

Now that you've decided to use your intuition start by doing a reality check with your closest relationships. If you are unclear whether it's a pretend relationship or a real one, take a deep breath, be brave, and ask someone. And not just anyone. Every person has that friend who will be honest with them no matter what. They are the ones who play devil's advocate. These friends are usually right. It's never fun to hear you may be wrong about

---

[3] The video link is in the resources.

something, but you have to be in touch with reality.

I was having a beer with my friend Allison, stressing about my lack of feelings. I hypothesized that maybe I'm a new breed of psychopath. One that doesn't experience real feelings, only fake ones since I cry during movies but usually not during normal times.

She said, "You have feelings; you just repress them."

I don't care if she is a psychologist and has been my best friend since I was sixteen; what does she know, right?

Grab a beer with that truth-telling friend and check-in with reality.

If you aren't up for that conversation yet, put it to paper. Writing out each of my relationships was a healthy way for me to understand and reflect back on how I function in them. Ask yourself these questions to help you write them out. How do I view them? How do I behave towards them? How do they behave towards me? What things could be affecting our perspectives? Don't feel you have to put them in a book as I did, but a good journal will do the trick.

Give yourself time for understanding your relationships. It doesn't come easy. I'm aware that there could have been some traumatic and horrific events in some relationships. In those cases Find a mental health counselor to talk with. You aren't alone in this. Having an unbiased third party can be extremely enlightening and helpful.

Learning to trust your intuition does not happen overnight. You already decided to grow as a person and understand your relationships. Be kind to yourself during this process. Trust it is working for your highest good.

There are useful tools to help you figure it out. Tools are the best way for beginners to trust themselves. They are an easy systematic approach to help understand and possibly confirm your intuition. Tarot or angel cards, for instance, work well and pendulums too. I use my own cards almost weekly for guidance. When I feel overwhelmed, I ask my sister-in-law to do a draw for me. It's simple and can usually create a sense of calm and clarity to help guide me. People even read tea leaves and can take pictures of your aura. There are all sorts of fancy readings and tools that enhance our journey towards trusting our intuition. Have fun and go experience a wide variety of them.

Step three: Ask

Ask your intuition/higher power/God/Universe for some help. I know it sounds elementary, but if you don't ask, you aren't going to get help. And don't ask some generic bullshit selfish question. *Can you help me win the lottery?* We need to ask specific questions. Questions with yes or no answers are best. Also, our intuition is always working for our best interest. So if we ask to win the lottery, what is our actual plan for that? Is that really going to get us to our higher purpose? For most people, the answer is no. They want to win it for a nice car, to pay off student loans, and get a new house. Philanthropy comes as an afterthought. We can't fool our intuition; it knows our subconscious plans even if we don't.

Here are some great questions to ask your intuition. Write them in your journal. Write them on a scrap piece of paper and put them in a basket for the Universe to carry away. You can even just say them out loud. Whatever feels right for you.

Career

"Am I making the right decision about staying at my job?"
"Should I look for another career?"
"Is this job the right one for me?"

Relationships

"Should I stay in my current relationship?"
"Is this relationship toxic for me?"
"Will this relationship progress where I want to go?"

Money

"What opportunities for abundance are out there for me?"
"Where should I look to find more money?"
"Can you send a sign about my next opportunity for abundance?"

Basic questions

"Can you send me a sign if I'm supposed to _____?"
"Is this the decision for my highest good?"

Write your own questions

Question:

Question:

Question:

Question:

Step four: Listen

This comes with practice. Mistakes will be made. It's okay. Nobody is perfect. I can't tell you exactly what your intuition sounds like or what it feels like. It's different for everyone. Here are the three best ways to listen.

Your feeling. Again this comes with practice. Think about the exercise I had you do earlier about listing the all the big deal choices. Think about the time you made those *mine* decisions. How did you feel during those times? You were likely in a state of flow or just going off that feeling of it being right. That's the feeling you want. Think about how it felt after you made that decision. Did it feel good and settled, or was there a bit of unexplainable unease?

Don't confuse normal unease about a decision with your intuitive sense of unease. Let's say you made a decision to move to a new town. Clearly there will be some anxiety and unease around that decision. But if you used your intuitive mind to make the choice, there shouldn't be that ache in your inner-self. Only practice and experience can help you know the difference.

For me, if a thought comes in, I check in with my gut. How am I feeling since I ignored it? Is that thought or feeling repeating? Can I do something about it? If I can, how do I feel after?

I had a two o'clock meeting with a publisher, so my husband had to work at home to watch our daughter. It would be very unlikely I would be done by three, so he would also have to pick up our son from school.

The meeting was going well, and I wasn't going to have time to pick up our son, so my husband would have to do it. No biggie. A little past three o'clock, in the middle of the meeting, a random thought popped in. *He forgot to pick him up.* Strange …

119

My husband had never done that before. So I went through the logic checkpoints: *I had mentioned to him that I would let him know if I could pick up our son. Since I haven't contacted him, he would know he had to.*

I dismissed the thought and refocused on being an active listener. But the nagging feeling that my husband forgot to pick him up persisted. I didn't want to be rude and check my phone, so again I just pushed them down. It was about 3:40 p.m. when I hopped into my car. I didn't have any messages or texts, which meant everything was fine. I called my husband to let him know I was on my way.

He picked up and said, "Hey, you on your way to pick him up?"

He forgot.

"Your fucking joking right? It's 3:40!"

Just then I got an incoming call from the school. *Ugh.*

I can't describe what intuition feels like, but I know how pissed I get when I don't listen to it. Even with practice, you'll learn to recognize the little intuitive feeling. Then you'll start to realize how light you feel when you do actually listen to it.

Your sign. Not your astrology sign. I'm talking about your sign from the Universe. The sign that lets you know you are where you are supposed to be and helps guide you when you ask questions. My sign from the Universe is purple. I often don't even ask for a sign, but I'll still receive one. I started a writing class, and as I walked in the instructor was wearing a purple scarf, purple blouse, and wrote with a purple pen. All of them were shiny to me. I instantly knew she was going to help me along my path.

I mentioned it earlier, but Gabrielle Bernstein has a wonderful method to find your sign from the Universe in her book *The Universe Has Your Back.* If there's a book to read after this one, it's that. I can't tell you how life-changing it was for me. In case you can't get her book, I've shared a link to her blog with the same information about picking your sign in the resources section. It's worth it.

Your dreams. If you have vivid dreams, or even if you don't, ask your question before you go to bed. Ask the same question every night for a week or two until you have a dream you can remember. With a bit of practice, you'll be able to interpret your dreams easily. Sometimes dreams are a mix and match of random shit that has happened recently. But often they reach into the deep coves of your subconscious and dig out the intuitive answer to your question. I have a dream dictionary next to my bed, so I look up any images I can remember before I forget. My friend Sam had suppressed her ability to see colors, which then started to manifest into vivid and creepily accurate dreams. When we have a purpose, it will do what it can to get through to us.

I use all three of these methods interchangeably. My feelings, my Universe sign, and my dreams. If you are just starting out, I would recommend picking the one that appeals to you the most—go with what feels right—and focus on understanding that before learning about another.

I personally love dreams the most. I use to have crazy nightmares. I can still remember nightmares I had as a child. I have multiple versions of recurring dreams. It wasn't until I started understanding how dreams work that I realized my dreams were messages. I no longer was afraid of my dreams. Now when I have nightmares, 90 percent of the time I'm aware that I'm dreaming and just handle it. I pull out the ratty old bra lesson even in my dreams and say: *Hey creepy, scary thing, I know you aren't real, so bugger off.* It's sort of fun now. I get to be my own hero in my dreams, or I receive some cool messages.

After I learned about my spirit guides, I asked if I could meet them in my dream. I asked a couple of nights before they finally came through. The dream was so vivid. I knew instantly that it was them. I walked into my old house. To my left a soft, blue glow from an old television bathed a dark-haired man in his mid-thirties. He just looked up, gave me a knowing head nod, and turned back to the glow of the television. To my right were two beautiful women. One was older with gray hair who sat at a grand piano. The other sat in front on a bench doing something with her hands, I don't remember exactly what. She was younger with long, dark hair. Both smiled at me, but nobody said anything. Nobody had to. It was a peaceful and comforting dream. I woke up so full of gratitude that they were willing to introduce themselves to me so clearly.

I love to sleep, but I fucking love dreaming!

Decide. Reality Check. Ask. Listen.

Only four steps but they are big ones. They take time. They take practice. They can all happen at the same time. You have to decide to leave your comfort zone and face reality. You have to be okay with not understanding fully or knowing if you are right. That is really how we can access our intuition and become more intuitive with our decisions and purpose. No special tie-dyed attire needed.

19

Bigger Purpose

W hy should we be listening to our intuition? Why can't we just make decisions with logic and reason? That seems easier than all this feelings stuff, right? Trust me, feelings are still icky for me. I still wonder if I'm not some sort of breed of psychopath that cries during movies or during any Adele song.

One reason to listen to our intuition is that today it's hard to know what the real story is. It's now on us to fact check and read beyond the headlines. Each news source takes its own view on a story, not leaving much room for us to decide for ourselves. Fox News ran a headline that stated: "Sean Spicer Ambushed by Woman in Apple Store." The same story was run by the *Washington Post*. "Sean Spicer Gets Confronted in Apple Store: Trump Responds."

They tell the same story but in two very dynamically different ways. Fox is setting up a fear-based story by using the word *ambushed*. The other is setting up the reader to see how Trump responded to it. If we are using our intuition, we can learn to read beyond the attention-grabbing words and intuitively know what the story is about. And since we rarely make it a priority to fact-check or use different sources of information to find out what the real story is, our intuition is a vital aspect of our worldview. It's important to listen to our intuition and be aware of it so we don't let headlines or people trying to get into our psyche make the decisions for us. Use your intuition to take back control and make the decisions for yourself.

Another reason for me to trust my intuition is that when death comes, I don't want to be the person with regrets. I want to be able to say: *I'm happy I went for it.* In the end, the only thing that matters is what is in your heart. I want my heart full of love. Love for myself, love for others. I don't think an easy life is one that can bring me all of that. I don't care if my life was easy; I care if I lived my life with purpose.

You may already have a happy, satisfying life. You probably could die comfortably, but still, there is something lingering within that can't be put into words. I firmly believe that little something is our intuition and the Universe trying to communicate with us.

I firmly believe every single person has a purpose bigger than themselves, and intuition is the thing to get us there. To get you there. Life is not about personal gain and glory; it's never about you. If the only reason you're doing good things is for your own benefit like getting to heaven, isn't that selfish? We should do nice things because it's the right thing to do and because it *feels* right when we do them. It feels right when we serve others because our purpose is never about us. Buy someone a coffee next time and pay attention to how you feel after. That's the sensation of a purpose higher than yourself.

I was at the dollar store the other day and a young man's debit card wasn't working. He insisted he just got paid and had the money in the account. The cashier asked him to stand aside until the manager came over. I noticed the amount due totaled three dollars. I handed the cashier the money. The young man couldn't believe I paid for his items. "That is was the nicest thing anyone has done for me."

A three dollar bill being paid was the nicest thing for him? That day, my purpose was to make sure that young man knew he was cared about. That feeling, people, is what true purpose feels like.

Mark Twain said, "The two most important days in your life are the day you were born, and the day you find out why."

Maybe our purpose changes, maybe we'll never understand exactly what our purpose is, but I do know I'm living my life purposefully. That day in the dollar store was my purpose. Fourteen years of service in the military was my purpose. That pile of ratty old bras was part of my purpose. And right now, this book is my purpose. I don't know what exactly this book was meant to do, but I trust that the Universe has my back and is only going to lead me with the highest good in mind.

So don't freak out if you don't know what your purpose is. You don't have to. If you're trusting and listening to your intuition, you're being led down that path already. There are times it may suck. Your path may crumble, shift, or come to an end. You may have a horrible break up. You may lose your house or job. You have to have faith. You have to listen to your intuition and trust it and know something bigger than you is at work.

I can't count how many people told me I was insane for leaving the military. I had more haters than supporters. I had a complete stranger literally call me stupid because I was giving up retirement money. I was not doing what society accepted as normal. But that little voice inside kept saying: *You've got this. You purpose is somewhere else now.*

In the end those are the only voices that matter. I couldn't ever be happy or live a life with no regrets if I didn't at least try to listen. I can't remember who or where I was, but someone told me: *Don't take advice from people you don't want to be.*

I'm not going to ask for financial advice from a gambler. I wasn't listening to career advice from those in the military because that wasn't for me anymore. I found people I aspired to be. Found people doing what I wanted to do and got advice from them.

People are always willing to give us advice. Solicited or not, people will always tell us what they think. Heck, I'm literally writing a book giving you my advice on intuition. We all do it. Just be cognizant of where you want to go.

Besides giving advice, people also love to complain, which can easily be mistaken for asking for help. I've come to learn that the ones who complain the loudest are the ones that want help the least. What they really want is pity. They want a pity party and an easy button. I've had to learn to trust my intuition to know the difference between someone complaining and someone that actually wants help. I can't waste time with those that complain. I can't let complainers bring me down with their pity party. Don't let people do that to you either. Get out of those conversations as fast as possible. I have an awesome purpose party rocking. Rock your purpose party and leave the haters at the door.

20

Socially Accepted

As you begin to talk about your intuition, you need some social awareness of your audience and where you're at. During my first holistic healing class, a fellow student stood up and introduced herself, "My name is Deborah and trees and rocks talk to me."

Oh Deborah. As possibly true as that could be, there are just so many things wrong with this approach. Maybe: *My name is Deborah and ever since I was little I've had a special connection with nature,* or *My name is Deborah and I love nature, especially rocks and crystals. They help me feel whole.* I mean the possibilities are endless of more socially acceptable approaches. Since it was a holistic class, maybe she thought it was okay to start that way. The place may have been right, but the audience was not. In a room full of people who don't know you, that's probably not the something to lead with.

Now, I've been known to use some offensive language. But I'm not going to introduce myself like I'm trying to get in the F-bomb hall of fame. If I'm presenting in a hospital or to a group of peers, I leave the military mouth at home.

If you just thought: *Oh, no; I'm socially awkward. I get nervous and always say the wrong thing.* Don't fret; I feel you. I once meant to tell my friends I need to stop at an ATM to get some money, but what came out was *I need to stop to get some monkeys.* We all are socially awkward at times and it's fine. It can make for a good story later.

Do you want to know the secret of being the most interesting person in any social setting? Ask questions and shut your mouth. Be curious and genuinely interested in learning about them. Never talk about yourself. That's it.

Even if they tell you how much they love mushrooms and how amazing they are, just keep the fact you would never eat those dirty, disgusting, fungi to yourself. They don't care. They just want to tell you about how much they care about (gag) mushrooms. Who knows? Maybe if you let them talk long enough, you'll learn an interesting fact about those nauseating forest funk morsels that you can later use to help eradicate them from the world.

Now if you really want to become socially awesome, here is where this question trick really works out. When you asked a question, since you weren't worried about responding with your story, you actively listened and more than likely you remembered what they said. So the next time you see them, you can impress them by asking how their kid's hockey game went or if they were able to visit the giant mushroom tree in that old brewery that they were raving about.

If all the questions you can think of are related to the weather or their job, don't worry, there is a plethora of great social questions to ask out in the world already. I love a journal I found by Picadilly titled *3000 Questions about Me.* Sure, they are great questions to ask yourself, but it's a gold mine for questions to ask in any social situation.

As your intuition grows, your confidence grows. You'll be amazed how often you can be in a social situation and walk up to the one random person that is from your hometown. Or went to the same college. Or whose kids are in the same school. Or who shares your love of the same comedian. Your intuition can do that for you. Once you find that common ground, you can relax, and over time your social anxiety may ease.

The more we as a society learn about mindfulness and expand our understanding of how the world works, the more intuition becomes recognized as an integral part of our well-being and success. Read any interview with entrepreneurs, business owners, or happy people and you'll find most experienced a moment when a clearly intuitive decision impacted their success. The History Channel series, *The Men Who Built America*, told a story about how John D. Rockefeller had to take a train for an important meeting with Cornelius Vanderbilt. Before getting on the train, he had a strong urge to go pray at church. As they were leaving the church, his carriage broke down, and he missed the train. He was upset and angry about missing a potentially huge business opportunity. He later learned the train he missed derailed, killing everyone on board. He had no reasonable, logical reason to go pray that night, but he did. His intuitive urge to stop at church saved his life.

As I have said before, we may never know if our intuition was right. We may never understand fully why we had that strong urge to download a book or ask a stranger a question. That's okay.

We owe nobody an explanation. When people ask why I wrote a book, I'm completely okay with saying: *Because my intuition guided me to do it.* I don't feel I need to justify it anymore than that.

I continually push past my comfort zone and do things I know feel right. Nothing in this book was in my comfort zone. Heck, the actual act of writing was not in my comfort zone. But I trusted my intuition. And I also know that just outside the comfort zone is fucking awesomeness. I'm addicted to that sense of discovering what is outside of my comfort zone. I love that uncertainty and sense of exploration. I want that feeling all the time. I want that more than society's acceptance. I want self-acceptance.

And here is the funniest fucking thing.

I have never—and I mean *never*—felt more accepted, loved, and satisfied than I do now. My intuition has led me to the most wonderful people. My intuition keeps providing me comfort when I step out of the comfort zone. Brené Brown, an author and research professor, says it's *braving the wilderness.* I feel I am myself when I am out in the wilderness.

I have more faith in myself and my capabilities than ever. I just wrote an entire book. This nobody, lisping, bunny destroyer wrote a book!

I credit all this to listening to my intuition. My path so far as led down some twists, curves, and has blown me full force out of the whale, but everything was done with a purpose. I either learned a lesson or it worked out as planned.

Harnessing our intuition is how we become socially accepted. It's how we can be happy with the path our life is on. We can have confidence in any situation or decision when we are using our intuition. Social acceptance isn't worrying about what people will think of us or fitting in. It's not about being normal. It's accepting our true self. When we accept ourself—our whole intuitive self—things fall into place and we'll know we are on the right path.

I didn't fit in small-town North Dakota. Not because of the people or because of who I am. I didn't fit in because my purpose was somewhere else. That unsettled, awkward feeling wasn't a judgment of myself or others. It was my intuition and the Universe trying to move me in line with my purpose. The ratty old bra lessons ended up being a gift from the Universe. The Universe knew I would be braving the wilderness, fighting off the saber-toothed tigers.

Decide to trust your intuition and live in reality. Ask for direction. Listen for the answer. There is always an answer. My reality is not perfect. I have issues and problems just as everyone else. I am trying to raise my kids not to be assholes. My shoulder is jacked up. I pee if I laugh too hard. My cat has arthritis. The struggles are real people. We all have problems. But by trusting our intuition, we can better learn to handle them. When we can learn to accept our full intuitive selves, things will begin to fall into place. Things will begin to feel right. My intuition has led me to a beautiful, purply world, balanced between crunchy and socially accepted. This world exists for you too. I know it's incredibly difficult to let go and let your intuition take the lead, but trust it. It's looking out for your best interest. Your intuition has always been with you. This superpower is right here, right now, waiting for you embrace it. You are and always will be—intuitive.

Resources and Recommended Readings

Recommended Readings:
Gabby Bernstein - *The Universe has Your Back & Judgment Detox*
Brené Brown - *Braving the Wilderness*
Elizabeth Gilbert - *Big Magic*
Michael Bodine – *Growing up Psychic*
Michael Lennox - *Llewellyn's Complete Dictionary of Dreams*

Learn more about:
- **Zack Anderson** - Tarot Readings https://www.eyeofhorus. biz/psychic-tarot/zack-anderson-tarot-reader
- **Gabby Bernstein** - Asking for Your Universe Sign https:// gabbybernstein.com/secret-asking-Universe-sign-trusting-guidance-receive
- **Tim Ferris** – Fear Setting https://tim.blog/2017/05/15/fear-setting
- **Marie Forleo** - Everything is Figureoutable. https:// marieforleo.com
- **Eric Post** – I wish my wife was ____ Relationship video: https://www.facebook.com/watch/?v=771459383024079
- **Laurie Wondra** -medium, energy worker, author, teacher and public speaker https://yourlifecore.com
- Docudrama – *The Men Who Built America* https://www. history.com/shows/men-who-built-america

- Documentary - ***The Most Unknown***
  https://www.themostunknown.com
- **Healing Touch** – Hands on energy healing www.healingbe-yondborders.org
- **Integrative Health & Healing Program** – Anoka-Ramsey Community College http://anokaramsey.edu
- **Dark matter**-What is Dark Matter? https://science.nasa.gov/astrophysics/focus-areas/what-is-dark-energy

About the Author

Socially Accepted Intuition is Rebecka Lassen's debut book. She shares her unique perspective on life and intuition through inspirational writing and speaking. She lives in North Saint Paul, Minnesota with her husband, two kids, two cats and a fish.

Join her monthly email newsletter for inspiration, humor, and updates on future publications.

If you wish to contact Rebecka, please write to her at the address below or through her website. She would appreciate hearing from you and learning about your experience with this book.

Please write to:

Rebecka Lassen
  P.O. Box 9264
  North St. Paul, MN 55109

Or find her online: www.rebeckalassen.com
  Instagram: www.instagram.com/becka_sai

Made in the USA
Middletown, DE
15 May 2019